Gooseberry Patch Co. SM

A Country Store In Your Mailbox

Welcome Home For The Holidays

From Harvest through Christmas...
a treasury of holiday recipes, decorating
tips, traditions & easy-to-make gifts!

Look for Vickie's & JoAnn's
favorite recipes and holiday hints
sprinkled throughout this book.

A Country Store In Your Mailbox ℠

Gooseberry Patch
27 N. Union St.
P.O. Box 190, Dept. WELC
Delaware, OH 43015

1-800-85-GOOSE
1-800-854-6673

Copyright© 1995, Gooseberry Patch
0-9632978-1-3
First Printing 30,000 copies, July 1994
Second Printing 30,000 copies, August 1994
Third Printing 50,000 copies, July 1995

How To Subscribe

Would you like to receive
"A Country Store in Your Mailbox ℠"?
For a 2-year subscription to our 72-page
Gooseberry Patch catalog,
simply send $3.00 to:
**Gooseberry Patch
27 N. Union St.
P.O. Box 190, Dept. WELC
Delaware, OH 43015**

Printed in the United States of America
TOOF COOKBOOK DIVISION

STARR ★ TOOF

670 South Cooper Street
Memphis, TN 38104

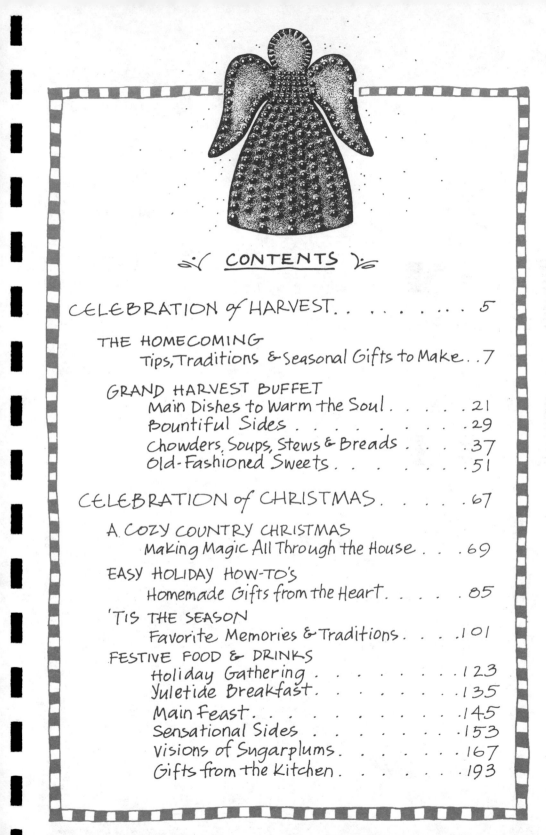

CONTENTS

CELEBRATION of HARVEST. 5

THE HOMECOMING
  Tips, Traditions & Seasonal Gifts to Make . . 7

GRAND HARVEST BUFFET
  Main Dishes to Warm the Soul. 21
  Bountiful Sides 29
  Chowders, Soups, Stews & Breads 37
  Old-Fashioned Sweets 51

CELEBRATION of CHRISTMAS. 67

A COZY COUNTRY CHRISTMAS
  Making Magic All Through the House . . . 69

EASY HOLIDAY HOW-TO'S
  Homemade Gifts from the Heart. 85

'TIS THE SEASON
  Favorite Memories & Traditions. . . . 101

FESTIVE FOOD & DRINKS
  Holiday Gathering 123
  Yuletide Breakfast. 135
  Main Feast. 145
  Sensational Sides 153
  Visions of Sugarplums. 167
  Gifts from the Kitchen 193

DEDICATION

To those who love hearth, home, and
holiday celebrations...
this book's for you!

IN APPRECIATION

A very special "Thanks"
to each and every one of you who helped
make this book a reality... may your holidays
be filled with happiness.

Celebration of Harvest

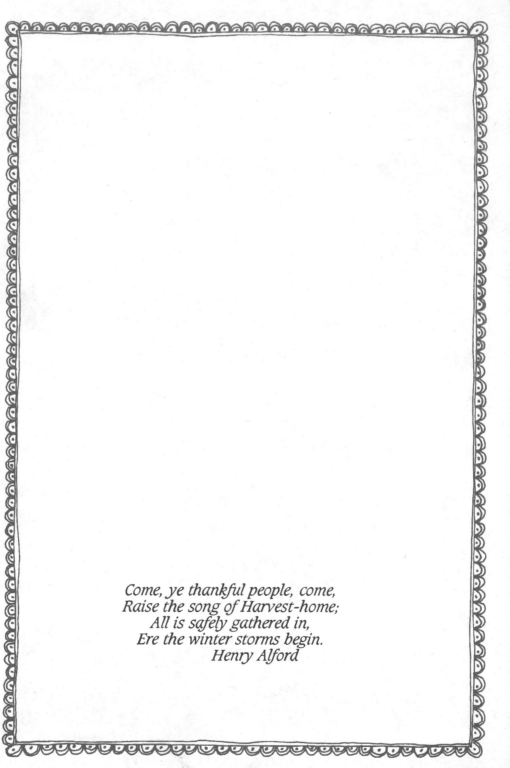

Come, ye thankful people, come,
Raise the song of Harvest-home;
All is safely gathered in,
Ere the winter storms begin.
Henry Alford

Tips, Traditions & Seasonal Gifts to Make

The Homecoming

For a wonderful holiday aroma and a delicious treat, take one gallon of apple cider and add 8-12 ounces of "red hots" or "cinnamon gems" in a crockpot. Stir until melted. Guests will want your recipe!

Denise Turner

This is a hint that goes back to my great grandmother and before there was ever a thought of a pre-basted turkey. Before you put your turkey in the oven, cover it with breakfast link sausages stuck on with toothpicks...the bird will look more like a porcupine than a turkey! Cover with foil and place in oven to roast. About 2 hours before serving, take off the foil and 30 minutes later take off the sausages (which are almost dried, and no longer greasy) and serve them as an appetizer. The bird will now get a beautiful golden brown and everyone will dive into the sausages. This has become a tradition at our house and never affects the taste of the turkey...just makes it extra juicy!

Wendy Lee Paffenroth

I love to decorate with gourds. They are beautiful arranged in a large basket with Indian corn and bittersweet for added color. After they are harvested (before frost), put them in a well ventilated place (I lay them on a side porch where they can be left alone). Turn them every few days while drying, which can take weeks or even months. I also wash off the mildew that collects on them with warm, soapy water and lay them back to dry (the mildew can make them look as though they are rotting). I know a gourd is good and dry when the mildew stops collecting on it. Washing with a disinfectant is also a good idea before bringing gourds into the house.

Martha Haught

Make cinnamon apple slices for use in potpourri, garlands or wreaths. All you need is:

8-10 apples	**6 t. cinnamon**	**1 t. cloves**
9 T. lemon juice	**2 t. allspice**	**2 t. arrow root powder**
2 t. salt		

Soak apples in juice for 6 minutes. Pat dry with paper towels. Toss in spices. You can dry apple slices in oven at 150-200 degrees for 6 hours; lay them out on waxed paper, turning once a day until dry; or dry in dehydrator.

Cheryl Ewer

Since moving into a 100 year old farmhouse and becoming an antique and auction buff, I'm always looking for ways to use my auction finds. A great way to use old seed bags that I found, was to make cushions for my porch swing and porch rockers. They look great and stand up to weather and many washings. To make cushions, use fiberfill by the yard, cut to fit the bag. Add ties to hold onto the chairs and tie with bright yarn, like you would do for a comforter.

Sandy Kolb

My favorite decorating idea for autumn involves my 14" jointed teddy bear, who perches in a chair in our front entryway. For harvest, he wears an orange "Lone Ranger" type mask and carries a 3-inch, tiny orange basket with stencilled jack-o'-lantern face, filled with colored fall leaves. In November he holds a miniature pumpkin on his lap with a scarecrow at his side. For Christmas, he sports a toddler's red toboggan and a 48 year old red sweater with real leather football buttons on it (this sweater belonged to my husband and is very sentimental to me). By his side is a little cloth bag filled with peppermint sticks and at his other side is a tiny child's picture book of a bear story . He is such a cheery greeting to me all day, every day of the year. I also place a "Muffy Bear" by the bannister rails of my stairway. In October she dresses in her black cat costume with a pumpkin. In November, she switches to her Pilgrim outfit, complete with pumpkin plus her very own turkey made out of felt and then changes to a snowman, with carrot nose for the holidays. They are so clever and fun!

Barbara Loe

I love autumn and Halloween but live in the country and get no trick-or-treaters so, I make my own! I collect teddy bears and dress up 5 or 6 of them to match the season...a devil, a skeleton, a witch, and so on. They sit on my hall tree and welcome visitors with a basket of Halloween candy. Funny, the candy always disappears by Halloween!

Kara Kimerline

Decorate a "welcome wreath" for your front door with giant sunflower heads, crows and bittersweet!

The Homecoming

We place sticks, leaves, mini pumpkins, gourds, and wooden fruit on our window sills during the fall season. It adds an autumn touch to the indoors!

Phyllis Ann Schantz

For me, autumn is a time to really make my house cozy. I like to buy several pumpkins, placing some on my front porch along with the potted plants and also throughout the table tops in my house. I also fill baskets with pretty fall leaves and small, colorful gourds and hang Indian corn, tied with raffia, on my front door and on the fireplace, giving a real "harvest" feel to the house. Candles in the holders and lamps change from pastels to dark, rich, autumn colors. Bowls are filled with fragrant potpourris and placemats and runners are changed to heavier weaves. I like to make Indian Spiced Tea as soon as the weather turns cold. Its wonderful fragrance fills the house and it tastes delicious. The tea keeps in the refrigerator for several days and can be reheated in the microwave or on the stove.

Indian Spiced Tea

6 c. cold water
12 whole cardamon pods
3- 2 1/2" to 3" cinnamon sticks,
    broken into pieces
3 T. Ceylon tea (any loose
    tea is fine)
3/4 c. sugar
2 c. milk

In a 3-quart pan, combine water, cardamon pods and cinnamon stick pieces. Bring to a boil over high heat; cover and continue boiling for 10 minutes. Add tea; return to a boil, then cover, reduce heat, and simmer for 2 to 3 minutes. Add sugar and milk; stir until sugar dissolves; cover and simmer for 3 to 4 minutes more. Strain through a fine sieve, discarding leaves and spices. Serve hot. Makes 6 servings.

Nancie Gensler

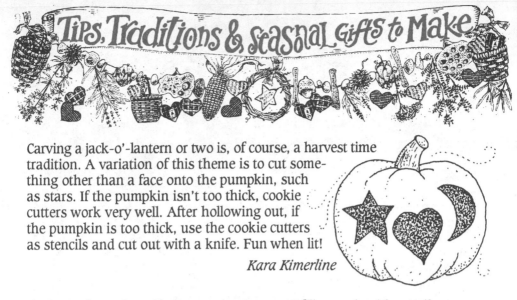

Carving a jack-o'-lantern or two is, of course, a harvest time tradition. A variation of this theme is to cut something other than a face onto the pumpkin, such as stars. If the pumpkin isn't too thick, cookie cutters work very well. After hollowing out, if the pumpkin is too thick, use the cookie cutters as stencils and cut out with a knife. Fun when lit!

Kara Kimerline

In September, when the leaves start to turn, I fill a crock with cattails, preserved oak leaves, and brown turkey feathers and set it on my kitchen pie safe. In October, the crock is joined by a large ceramic jack-o'-lantern (made by my mother), and a wooden black cat on wheels (like a pull toy). In November, the jack-o'-lantern is turned face to the wall, giving me a large ceramic pumpkin. Joining it is my collection of nutcrackers and a wicker cornucopia filled with a dried flower bouquet. I fill in empty spots with pinecones, gourds and bittersweet sprigs. In the living room, I fill baskets with wooden acorns, gourds and pinecones. The corner cupboard is filled with redware pottery and small baskets. Among the baskets I place more pinecones, gourds, small wooden pumpkins and bittersweet sprigs.

Gail Hageman

At the beginning of Fall each year, I hang stuffed cross-stitch ornaments, which I have done up in autumn designs, on a peg rack in my front entryway. I also hang a few coordinating candles next to them. Then right after Thanksgiving, I switch these ornaments for a few done in Christmas designs, and I hang forest green and deep wine colored candles. This is such a fun way for me to decorate with the seasons, and at the same time, display my handiwork.

Mariann Smith

I like to use my collections of teapots, fine china, colored glass, and silver items to decorate my end tables in my living room. I also use candles the colors of the season to add color to my display. A dish of potpourri, old-fashioned postcards, and my dolls dressed for the season add special touches. It looks inviting and many afternoons are spent enjoying a cup of tea and a good book.

Nancy Rootland

The Homecoming

Since early childhood, autumn has brought an excitement for me that no other season has been able to match. Perhaps it's because I was born in October that the end of summer holds no sadness, but instead brings with it a flood of anticipation for the autumnal delights that await. Autumn begins to stir in my soul around the middle of September and I can no longer wait to decorate! I bring out all the fall wreaths and a trip to the local produce market provides a bounty of pumpkins, gourds, squashes, plus the always needed Indian corn, to bring fall indoors. By late summer in eastern Tennessee, the leaves are shedding their green coats for golden yellows, burnished oranges and brilliant reds. I gather these treasures of fall before an early frost can claim them. They are brought indoors where they nestle among bowls of miniature pumpkins, gourds, squashes and Indian corn and tucked on shelves and inside cupboards filled with antiques.

In late September I decorate my artificial 4 1/2-ft. pine tree with one string of miniature, clear lights, honeysuckle vines, brown leaves, spider webbing, several spiders and miniature corn. Around the base of the tree I place a Halloween tree skirt and scatter fall leaves, pumpkins, gourds, squashes and Indian corn. Next, I place my antique jack-o'-lanterns, witches, scarecrows and noisemakers among the fall treasures. The local produce market provides small bales of hay upon which I perch some of my Halloween collectibles, which also include rare Halloween postcards. The display is finished off with a haunted house and graveyard that light up. The neighborhood children love it and it's a special treat for all the kids who come on Halloween night.

When Halloween is over, the tree is decorated for Thanksgiving, out come the pilgrims and turkeys! After Thanksgiving, the tree is decorated for Christmas and when the holidays are over, I decorate the tree with crocheted snowflakes and my snowman collection. The Christmas skirt is put away and a lace tablecloth takes its place. An antique sled adds to the scene and provides an excellent perch for snowmen. In February, the tree is decorated with lace trim and antique hearts for Valentine's Day. I love making use of my tree for six months out of the year. I never get tired of the warm glow of lights that give a special coziness to the house. Many of my decorations have come from Gooseberry Patch and fit in so nicely with my antiques.

Martha Haught

12

Tips, Traditions & Seasonal Gifts to Make

Make small bales of straw, hay, and alfalfa to decorate your porch, mantels and shelves. Stuff the straw into a cardboard milk carton, pack tightly, tie twine around the carton and when securely tied, tear away the carton. Makes a unique addition to fall arrangements along with your pumpkins and gourds.

Joyce Newburn

Make a birdseed wreath that our feathered friends would love, using one can of refrigerated bread stick dough, birdseed and one egg white. Separate dough into individual pieces. Dip each piece in egg white and roll in birdseed, pressing the loose seeds firmly into the dough. Over a lightly greased cookie sheet, form each piece into desired shape...hearts and circles work well. Pinch the ends together. Bake as directed on dough can. When cool, make hangers for wreaths from festive ribbon that can be tied onto wreath and then to tree branches, or nailed to a fence. Looks nice on outside pine trees with a popcorn garland.

Kara Kimerline

When we trim our grapevines in February, we use the vines to make grapevine wreaths and arches. After soaking the vines in water in the wading pool, we shape the wreaths and then they are hung to dry. After harvesting and drying flowers from my garden, I decorate the grapevine wreaths and arches. There is nothing more beautiful and personally fulfilling than what you can make with your own hands.

From our strawberry bed, grape arbor and vegetable garden, we make jams, jellies and hot sauce and put them in fancy little jars. I also purchase honey and special popcorn harvested locally in Iowa. These items are then used in gift baskets for neighbors and friends at Christmas and throughout the year for birthdays.

Nancy McGrew

Roasted Pumpkin Seeds
2 c. seeds   1 T. oil   1/2 t. salt

Rinse pumpkin seeds and dry on paper towel. Toss with oil and place on cookie sheet. Bake at 350 degrees for 20 minutes, tossing every 5-7 minutes, until golden. Remove from oven, salt and enjoy!

The Homecoming

This homemade seasoning mix is wonderful...will season anything. Makes a nice gift when packaged in a small jelly jar with a pretty top. Every year my friend grows and dries the herbs and I grow and then dry the chopped veggies in my dehydrator. Mix together and blend any or all of the following:

Vegetables:
onion (large amount)
celery (large amount)
carrot (moderate amount)
pepper (moderate amount)
tomato (smaller amount)

Herbs:
basil   thyme
bay leaf   parsley
sage   rosemary
oregano   garlic (if you like)

Sara Walker

For Thanksgiving I like to bake homemade sugar cookies, wrap them in colored plastic wrap (yellow and red, together), and tie with coordinating ribbon. I put them on a huge copper tray in the dry sink, by the front door, for my guests to take home.

Sally Kennedy

Our church replaces Halloween celebrations with a "Harvest Party", involving seasonal activities and fun. One great success has been the "Autumn Obstacle Course", in which the kids climb over hay bales, bob for apples and dash through cornstalks. It's fun to do and fun to watch!

Karen Hayes

There's one traditional part of our Thanksgiving meal that has never changed. Sometime during the meal each one of us shares with the others what they are thankful for.

Lois Eisenhut

14

My mom, Helen Love, swears this tea cures colds!

Mom's Cure-All Spice Tea Mix

2/3 c. instant tea
1 c. powdered orange drink mix
1/2 c. sugar
1/4 t. ground cloves
2 T. powdered lemonade mix
1/2 t. ground cinnamon

Mix all ingredients together; place mix in container.
To use, mix 2 teaspoons of mix per cup of boiling water.

Jeanne Elmer

For a pretty but different table decoration, try using miniature pumpkins or apples as candle holders. Just cut a small hole in the top of either and insert the candle. They look great with fall leaves and bittersweet for a harvest table, or fresh greens and small pinecones for a Christmas table.

Suzanne Carbaugh

We live in a town with a large university that has many foreign students who can't get home for the holidays. We "adopt" one of these students for the Thanksgiving holidays (we're going to try Christmas this year too). My three sons love this and so does the student. This year we had a Japanese girl stay with us and I don't know who benefited the most, her or my family. The joy that she brought us was immeasurable!

Suzy Roberts

Place a candy corn in each finger of a clear, plastic glove. Fill with popcorn and tie opening in glove with orange and/or black yarn. Put a plastic spider ring on the ring finger, and you have an adorable party favor for your child's Halloween parties.

Patty Sue Cooper

The Homecoming

I love the harvest season! We grow our own big pumpkins to carve jack-o'-lanterns for Halloween, roast the seeds and save some for next year's crop. It's also fun to decorate pumpkins with paints, markers and different materials. We also grow our own sweet corn, enjoy it during the summer and come autumn, use the cornstalks to decorate the lamp posts along with pumpkins, mums, bales of hay and a scarecrow. Fresh herbs taste wonderful and we have an abundance of basil and parsley in our garden. We make many batches of pesto, freeze and savor it during the winter months. From our grapevines, we make wreaths for the fall, along with the wild bittersweet we collect in a nearby field. We like to decorate our table for fall parties with a hollowed out sugar pumpkin shell filled with pumpkin soup or dip. On Halloween day, we make caramel candy apples dipped in flaked coconut and chopped peanuts and give them to our favorite trick-or-treaters. Another favorite fall event, our family goes apple picking at a nearby orchard. We always have plenty of apples throughout the season for candy apples, apple pies and applesauce. We also buy cider at the orchard for making hot mulled cider. A favorite past time for our family is to ride around looking at the fall foliage. It's even better to go for a hike through the brilliant colors and take photographs.

Joanne Jacobellis

Our children are 27, 19 & 16...really too old for trick-or-treating, but we still do! We call it "Harvest Day." The two oldest are married and live here on our farm. If anyone wants their treats, they have to dress up and come ring our bell. The treats aren't elaborate (baseball cards, little trinkets) and, of course, a little candy too. We carve a pumpkin, make caramel apples and enjoy baked treats. Our time spent together is so enjoyable. I act outlandishly silly, but no one has run me off yet!

Barbara Loe

Easy Apple Dumplings

Core apple and stuff with brown sugar and butter. Set apple on a square of already-prepared pie dough, brush all four sides with mixture of egg yolk and water and bring four edges of pie dough to top of apple. You can also cut out fall leaf designs with cookie cutters, brush with egg yolk mixture and decorate outside of pastry. Bake according to pie dough instructions.

Here's a yummy spiced cider mix to warm you up! Combine and store in airtight container:

Spiced Cider Mix

3/4 c. brown sugar
2 t. ground cinnamon
1 t. ground cloves
1/2 t. grated orange peel
1 t. ground allspice
1/2 t. ground nutmeg (if desired)

To make cider:
1/4 c. mix
1 c. apple juice
1/4 c. water

Combine mix, juice and water. Bring to a boil over medium heat, reduce heat and simmer for 5 minutes. Yield: 1 serving. Can also be made using red wine in place of apple juice.

Michelle Golz

I have a special secret hill that I go by in my car each day. In the fall, I harvest all the flower seed from my garden and then visit "my hill" in the spring, broadcasting my seed. People are surprised to see "wild" coxscomb, celosia, marigolds, columbine...just to name a few. You could also save the seed in jars, to use as gifts for others who may have special hills or yards.

Lisa Harmon

The church my husband and I were members of, before we moved, threw a Fall's Fest one year between Halloween and Thanksgiving. We offered stews, soups, chili, baked bread, biscuits, cornbread and had lots of desserts. During the evening we played games, took family pictures and ate! We decorated the family center in traditional fall decor...scarecrows, apples, pumpkins and quilts. We charged every person who attended one can of food, and at the end of the evening we made Thanksgiving baskets for selected families.

Glenette Schantz

The Homecoming

Each Thanksgiving, I set my table with little paper medicine cups holding 5 kernels of Indian corn by each place setting. When we sit down to our dinner, I read the following:

"The Legend of the Five Kernels"

The first winter, the Pilgrims spent in their new home was very cold. Food was in short supply. Some days they only had enough food for each person to have five kernels of corn for the day. But spring came. They planted food. It grew. And all the Pilgrims did not die.

From then on, when Thanksgiving came around, the Pilgrims put five kernels of corn on each plate to remind themselves of their blessings.

Let us remember:

The first kernel reminds us of the autumn beauty around us.
The second kernel reminds us of our love for one another.
The third kernel reminds us of God's love and care for us.
The fourth kernel reminds us of our friends...especially our Indian brothers.
*The fifth kernel reminds us we are a free people. **

Then we say our prayer and enjoy our meal.
*Story from the book, **Thanksgiving Handbook** by Ruth Odor. Children's Press, Chicago 1984.

Donna Whiteside

On Thanksgiving Day after dinner, our family always takes a walk through the woods and collects firewood to be used in our fireplace, for the first family fire of the season.

Each year at Thanksgiving, our family writes what they are thankful for in a special Thanksgiving card. They are careful not to view what the others have written. This special card is then read aloud on Thanksgiving Day.

Nancy Rootland

Start your own fall tradition by having a pumpkin carving party for children and adults alike. Have each person bring his/her own pumpkin and ice cream scoop (as this is the best tool for cleaning the inside of a pumpkin). Serve cider and doughnuts. Have acrylic paints and brushes on hand for the younger children to paint their pumpkins. Before lighting, remember to sprinkle the inside of your pumpkin with ground cinnamon and cloves for a wonderful scent.

Sharon Andrews
Gooseberry Patch Artisan

During the summer, when our pumpkins in the garden are about the size of large grapefruits, each member of our family selects his or her favorite. We then lightly carve our name into the pumpkins with a nail. It's fun to watch your pumpkin grow as your name becomes permanently etched into its surface. At harvest time we put our "family" of pumpkins on the front porch to greet visitors. The smaller ones can be taken in and displayed indoors.

Buy a bay plant at your local nursery. It will thrive on a sunny porch or deck all summer and when the weather turns cool, bring it inside and keep it on a sunny windowsill in your kitchen. Whenever you make soup or stew, pinch off a leaf or two and add to the pot. So flavorful!

Barbara Bargdill
Gooseberry Patch

The Homecoming

My mother enjoys cooking and baking and we both love to celebrate the holidays. At Halloween, we host "The Great Pumpkin Dinner" (named by my brother), which our family anxiously anticipates.

The house is decorated inside and out with antique and new Halloween decorations we have gathered over the years. Handmade teddy bears dressed in Halloween costumes, sewn by my mother, greet visitors. A large orange tree in the parlor is lit with miniature pumpkin lights, and a dried hydrangea arrangement (from our garden) is set on the buffet in the dining room. Baskets of gourds are placed in every room. The table is set with a brown and white checked tablecloth, matching napkins, wooden napkin rings, and pewter candlesticks with orange candles. Brown stoneware dishes are accompanied by pewter wine and water goblets. Our centerpiece is marigolds and mums cut from our garden and arranged in a basket or pumpkin container.

The "Great Pumpkin Dinner" menu is as follows: Pumpkin stew (beef stew cooked and served in a pumpkin shell); string beans (fresh, if possible); tossed salad with choice of dressings; homemade pumpkin muffins, biscuits, and cornmeal sticks; apple crisp; pumpkin cake roll; Halloween mints and foiled chocolates, apple cider and hot steaming coffee. The "Great Pumpkin Dinner" has been a tradition in our family for many years...one of the many traditions we all look forward to.

Eileen Curran

Main Dishes To Warm The Soul

Pasta Fagiola

*David L. Bamford
(JoAnn's Dad)*

This "pasta soup" is hearty and satisfying!

olive oil
6-8 cloves garlic
1 chopped carrot
1 stalk chopped celery
1/4 c. chopped celery leaves
1/2 lb. thickly sliced diced
  prosiutto
2- 28 oz. cans Italian plum
  tomatoes

1 t. basil
1 t. oregano
1 t. rosemary
pinch of crushed red pepper
3- 19 oz. cans white
  cannelini beans
2 cans water
ditalini (type of pasta)

Cover bottom of a large soup pot with olive oil and saute garlic, carrot, celery, leaves, and prosiutto. Saute 15-20 minutes until celery and carrots are soft. Add tomatoes broken up with your hands. Add herbs and spices, beans and water. Cook 1-2 hours until soup thickens. Serve over ditalini.

Pasta al Pesto

Joanne A. Jacobellis

2 c. loosely packed fresh
  basil leaves, chopped
1 c. fresh Italian parsley,
  chopped (flat leaves)
1/2 t. salt
2 medium cloves garlic,
  chopped
1/4 c. walnuts
1/2 c. fresh grated
  parmesan cheese

2 t. fresh lemon
  juice
1 small tomato,
  chopped
3/4 c. olive oil
1 lb. pasta (very
  thin spaghetti),
  cooked

In blender, combine basil, parsley, salt, garlic, nuts, cheese and lemon juice. Process until mixture is a thick paste, slowly blend in tomato. Add oil, a little bit at a time, until oil is totally absorbed into mixture. Pour over hot pasta.

Main Dishes To Warm The Soul

Barbecue Beef

Janet Schaeper
(Vickie's sister)

Great for big family get-togethers, tailgate parties or fundraising events. Everyone loves a hot barbecue beef sandwich!

6 lbs. beef (chuck or stew)
1 stalk celery (chopped)
3 large onions (chopped)
1 green pepper (chopped)
1 medium bottle ketchup
3 T. barbecue sauce

3 T. vinegar
1 T. chili powder
2 T. salt
1 t. pepper
1 1/2 c. water

Cut beef into chunks, place in roaster or dutch oven. Combine all other ingredients. Pour over the meat. Heat to boiling on top of range. Cover and either simmer or bake in a 300 degree oven for 6 hours or until the meat will shred with a fork. (I cook mine in a pressure cooker for 50 minutes). If too soupy, cook uncovered a little longer until the right consistency to spoon onto buns. Serves 40.

Smoked Sausage Harvest Casserole

Linda Tittle

2 T. margarine
5 c. chopped green cabbage
1 onion, cut in halves and sliced
1 c. sliced carrots
1 can (15 1/2 oz.) drained red
    beans (optional)

1 can (8 oz.) stewed tomatoes
1 T. vinegar
1/3 c. grated parmesan cheese
2 T. flour
dash of black pepper
1 lb. lite smoked sausage

Heat oven to 350 degrees. Melt margarine over medium-high heat. Add cabbage, onion and carrots; saute for 5 minutes. Stir in beans, tomatoes and vinegar. Sprinkle cheese, flour and pepper over cabbage mixture, then stir. Spoon into a greased shallow 2-quart casserole. Cut sausage into serving pieces and arrange on top of cabbage mixture, pushing them down partially. Cover and bake for 40 minutes or until hot. Serves 6.

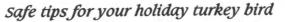

Safe tips for your holiday turkey bird

• *Thaw in the microwave or refrigerator.*
• *Don't cook overnight at low temperatures. Cook at 325 degrees.*
• *After it's cooked, don't leave it sitting out for more than 2 hours.*

◆ Grand Harvest Buffet ◆

Those Harvest Meatballs

Elenna Firme
Gooseberry Patch Artisan

I first tried this recipe for wheat harvest when I took large meals out to the field. It was supposed to be meat loaf, but I thought it would look nicer to serve as big meatballs. They were a big hit and have been ever since for harvest, picnics and potluck dinners. I have never changed an ingredient or made it into meat loaf!

1 1/2 to 2 lbs. ground beef
1/4 t. chili powder
1/2 c. ketchup
2 eggs
1/2 c. milk
1 t. prepared mustard
1 t. salt
chopped onion
pepper to taste

1 t. beef bouillon
1 t. worcestershire sauce
1/2 c. bread crumbs, fine
1/2 c. oatmeal

Sauce:
1/2 c. ketchup
1/2 c. brown sugar
1 t. prepared mustard

Heat oven to 350 degrees. Mix all ingredients together well. Form portions into large 2 1/2"-3" balls and place in a 13"x9" baking dish. Bake for 30 minutes. Carefully blot each meatball on paper towels to eliminate all the drippings. Replace in another clean 13"x 9" baking dish. Pour the following sauce over the meatballs and bake another 15 minutes. For fancier occasions, you can make small 1" balls. Reduce cooking time. Then put in a chafing dish to serve.

Reuben Casserole

Joyce Newburn

1 bag sauerkraut, drained
1/2 lb. Swiss cheese
1 can corned beef
1 small bottle Thousand Island
   dressing
rye bread crumbs (for the top)

Layer all ingredients (except bread crumbs and salad dressing), alternating each (so that you get 2 layers of each ingredient). Pour dressing over and put bread crumbs on top. Bake in a greased 13"x9" baking dish at 350 degrees for 1 hour.

Dinner-In-A-Pumpkin

Juanita Williams

This is a perfect Halloween "make-ahead" dinner for that busy trick or treat evening!

1 (8 to 10 lb.) pumpkin
1 1/2 lbs. ground beef
1 small onion, chopped
1 clove garlic, minced
1 1/2 t. sugar
1 1/2 t. mixed Italian herbs
1 1/2 t. salt
1/8 t. pepper
4 c. tomato juice
3 c. cabbage, shredded
1/2 lb. green beans
1 c. rice, uncooked

Wash pumpkin, cut off top and scrape out seeds and discard. Cook ground beef slightly; drain off fat. Add onion and garlic, saute slightly. Add seasonings and tomato juice; heat. Mix with uncooked rice. Shred cabbage and cut green beans. Layer 1/3 each of the cabbage, green beans, rice and meat mixture in pumpkin. Repeat layers and replace lid. Bake at 350 degrees for 2 1/2 to 3 hours or until done. Pumpkin is done when it is soft when pierced with a fork. Serve with tossed green salad and cornbread.

Grand Harvest Buffet

Chicken-Rosemary Casserole

Gail Hageman

Delicious served with rolls and a salad!

3 c. cooked, diced chicken
8 oz. raw macaroni
2- 10 3/4 oz. cans cream of
mushroom soup
2 c. milk

1/2 lb. grated cheddar cheese
1 oz. jar pimientos, chopped
1 T. chopped onion
1 t. salt
1 t. dried rosemary or 2 t. fresh

Mix all ingredients together. Let stand overnight in refrigerator (6 to 8 hours). Mix and spoon into deep 2-quart casserole dish. Bake at 350 degrees for 1 to 1 1/4 hours. Serves 4-6.

Cheddar Chicken Pot Pie

Gail Hageman

1 ready pie crust
1 1/2 c. chicken broth
2 c. peeled, cubed potatoes
1 c. sliced carrots
1/2 c. sliced celery
1/2 c. chopped onion
1/4 c. all-purpose flour

1 1/2 c. milk
2 c. (8 oz.) shredded cheddar
cheese
4 c. diced, cooked chicken
1/4 t. poultry seasoning
salt and pepper to taste

Heat broth to a boil in dutch oven. Add vegetables and simmer 10-15 minutes or until tender. Blend flour with milk, stir into broth mixture. Cook and stir over medium heat until slightly thickened. Stir in cheese, chicken and poultry seasoning, salt and pepper. Heat until cheese melts. Spoon into a 10" (2 1/2 to 3-quart) casserole. Place crust over filling in casserole. Seal edges. Make several slits in crust for steam. Bake at 425 degrees for 40 minutes or until golden. Yield: 6 servings.

An' all us other children, when the supper things is done,
We set around the kitchen fire an' has the mostest fun
A-list'nin' to the witch-tales 'at Annie tells about,
An' the Gobble-uns 'at gits you Ef you don't watch out!
James Whitcomb Riley

Main Dishes To Warm The Soul

Sour Cream Tacos

Neta Liebscher

3 c. diced, leftover turkey (one chicken fryer can be
  boiled and deboned)
1 pt. sour cream
1 lb. American cheese, shredded
2- 14 1/2 oz. cans tomatoes, cut up
1 large onion, chopped
2 T. oil
1 to 2 c. chicken broth
4 to 6 canned jalapeno peppers,
  chopped
1 t. salt
1/2 t. pepper
12 corn tortillas, torn into
  small pieces
1 c. cheddar cheese, grated

Saute onions in oil, add chicken
broth, jalapeno peppers, salt and
pepper. Mix turkey, sour cream,
American cheese, and tomatoes. Add
onion mixture to turkey mixture, along with
the "torn" tortillas; mix well. Place in a 13"x9"
baking pan. Bake at 350 degrees for 30-40 minutes.
The last 10 minutes of baking, top with the cheddar cheese. Serves 6.

Russian Mushroom Pie

Alfreda Crosley

Delicious served as an appetizer cut into small wedges with crackers, or as
a main course.

3 T. butter
1/4 c. chopped onions
1 lb. fresh mushrooms, sliced
2 t. flour

1/2 c. parmesan cheese
1 egg, well beaten
1 c. sour cream

Saute onion in butter; add mushroom and cook about 8 minutes. Sprinkle
in flour and add parmesan cheese. Cook 1 minute. Beat egg and sour cream
together and set aside. Pour mushroom mix into an 8" buttered pie plate;
top with sour cream mixture. Bake 20 minutes at 350 degrees.

Harvest Quiche

Serve as a luncheon dish with a crisp salad and chilled white wine.

Crust:

1 1/4 c. sifted all-purpose flour
pinch of salt
3 T. butter

3 T. shortening
3 to 4 T. cold water

Sift the flour and salt together. Cut the butter and shortening into the flour with a pastry blender or two knives until it resembles coarse meal. Add three tablespoons water and mix with a fork and then your fingertips until the dough can be gathered into a ball. If the dough is very crumbly, sprinkle a few drops of water over the dough, adding only enough to make the dough stick together. Wrap the dough in waxed paper and chill in the refrigerator (at least one hour) before rolling out. Roll out on a floured board and fit into a 9 to 10 inch quiche tin or 9 inch pie plate. Cover the pastry with a sheet of aluminium foil, pressing it firmly around the sides and over the edges of the pastry. Fill with uncooked rice or dry beans and bake in preheated 400 degree oven for 7 minutes. Carefully remove the rice or beans and aluminium foil. Prick the bottom of the crust with a fork and continue baking 5 minutes more. The crust should not brown but should be only partially baked. Let the pastry cool before filling and baking quiche.

Filling:

1/2 lb. cooked chicken breast,
    cut into small cubes
1 c. grated Swiss cheese
1/2 c. apples, cut into small cubes

1/2 t. cinnamon
2 T. Madeira (optional)

Scatter the chicken, cheese and apples over the bottom of the pastry shell and sprinkle with cinnamon. Stir the optional Madeira into the custard mixture and pour over the chicken, cheese and apples. Bake in preheated 375 degree oven for 40 minutes until custard is puffy and brown. Serves 6.

Custard:

4 eggs
3/4 c. milk
3/4 c. heavy cream
pinch of nutmeg (freshly grated,
    if possible)

1 T. flour
2 T. melted butter
pinch of salt
pinch of cayenne pepper

Beat all ingredients together with a wire whisk until blended.

Bountiful Sides

✦ Grand Harvest Buffet ✦

Corn Custard

Cindy Patrick

2 c. corn kernels
   (preferable frozen)
1 T. sugar
2 T. flour
1/2 t. cornstarch

3/4 t. dry mustard
3 eggs, well beaten
2 c. milk
1 T. worcestershire sauce
2 T. melted butter

Mix corn and dry ingredients. Add eggs, milk, worcestershire and butter. Blend well. Bake in a 2 quart buttered casserole (set inside a larger pan filled with hot water). Bake at 350 degrees for 50-60 minutes or until knife comes out clean.

Old Settlers' Baked Beans

Connie Himmelberger

1 can pork & beans
1 can butter beans
1 can kidney beans
1/2 lb. bacon, browned and
   cut into 1" pieces

1 lb. hamburger, browned
1/2 c. sugar
1/2 c. brown sugar
1/4 c. ketchup
1 t. mustard

Combine ingredients and cook on low in your crockpot for 6 hours or so. Serve warm with cornbread. Serves 6 people or more.

Harvest Salad

Kay Redd

Gets creamier and tastes better the longer it sits!

1 head lettuce, cut up
1 head cauliflower, cut up
1 large onion, diced
1 lb. bacon, fried and broken
   into small pieces
8 oz. shredded mozzarella cheese
1 pt. mayonnaise (do not use salad
   dressing)

Combine in a large container. Refrigerate.

Maple Candied Sweet Potatoes

Josephine Lake

Simple and very good with turkey, pork or ham.

3 lbs. sweet potatoes
1/2 c. maple syrup
1/2 c. brown sugar
    (either light or dark)

2 T. butter
1/2 t. salt

Pare, halve and cook sweet potatoes in boiling salted water until tender (30-40 minutes). Cut into 1" slices. In saucepan, combine syrup, sugar, butter and salt; bring to a boil and simmer for 5 minutes. Place sweet potato slices in a 11"x7" baking pan. Spoon syrup over to coat. Bake uncovered at 350 degrees for 30 minutes, basting frequently. Serves 8-10.

Cranberry Orange Salad

Judy Carter

1 lb. fresh cranberries
1 c. sugar

juice of 1/2 lemon
1 orange

Grind cranberries and orange. Mix with sugar and juice. Refrigerate overnight.

Mini pumpkins can be roasted whole and used as single serving dishes. Puncture each pumpkin with a fork, bake on a baking sheet in the middle of a 350 degree oven until tender, about 1 hour. Hollow out and seed after roasting and fill with a mixture of cooked rice or steamy soup. Be sure and don't overbake your pumpkins so your "dishes" hold up well.

·Grand Harvest Buffet·

Broccoli Salad
Kay Redd

1 pkg. fresh or frozen broccoli,
   chopped into bite-sized pieces
1 sweet onion, chopped
1/2 c. grated cheddar cheese
1/2 lb. bacon

Dressing:
1/2 c. mayonnaise-type
   salad dressing
1/4 c. sugar
1 T. vinegar

Fry bacon and drain. Crumble and mix with broccoli, onion and cheese.
Add dressing just before serving. Best if does not sit.

Lentils and Rice
Kathy Bolyea

2 2/3 c. water
1 T. liquid beef bouillon
1 1/2 c. shredded cheese, any kind

3/4 c. dry lentils
1/2 c. chopped onion
1/2 c. brown rice

Combine all ingredients in a greased casserole dish. Bake covered at 350
degrees for 1 1/2 hours. Serves 4.

Apple Butternut Squash Casserole
Connie Carmack

2 lbs. fresh butternut squash, peeled and cubed
20 oz. can apple pie filling
1/2 t. pumpkin spice seasoning
1/2 t. nutmeg
3/4 t. salt
1 T. butter or
   margarine

Peel squash, cut into 2"
cubes and place in a
greased casserole. Top
with apple pie filling.
Sprinkle with season-
ings and dot with butter.
Cover with foil and bake
at 350 degrees for 50-60
minutes. Serves 6.

Bountiful Sides

Harvest Dressing
Linda Lockwood

2 apples, cored and chopped
1/2 c. golden raisins
1/2 c. chopped (coarsely) nuts, preferable walnuts or pecans
3 T. butter
1/4 c. brown sugar (more if sweeter dressing is desired)
2 c. whole wheat bread cubes
apple juice or cider

Saute apples and raisins in butter, add nuts, sugar and bread cubes. Add enough juice to moisten to desired texture. Bake in a 2-quart casserole dish at 400 degrees for 20-30 minutes. Serve as a side dish with pork or poultry.

Creamed Cucumber Salad
Susan Kirschenheiter

This is a very easy recipe. Great for when you benefit from the neighbor's endless harvest of cucumbers!

1 1/2 to 2 cucumbers, sliced paper thin
1 small diced onion (1" diameter onion)
1 small clove of garlic (or shakes of garlic powder)
1 t. salt

Let above sit in refrigerator for 1 hour. Squeeze out the juice and water and then add:

1/2 c. half-and-half
1 1/2 T. vinegar
1/2 t. pepper
1/2 t. paprika

Mix together, chill and serve.

Corn Casserole

Frances A. Harper

2 c. cream style corn (1 can)
1 box corn muffin mix (7 1/2 oz.)
3 eggs
1/2 c. oil

1/2 t. garlic powder
2 T. chopped pimiento
1/4 c. chopped green pepper
1 c. shredded cheddar cheese

Mix all ingredients, except cheese. Pour into a greased deep casserole dish (I usually use a 3-quart dish). Top casserole with the shredded cheese. Bake at 350 degrees for 45 minutes. Yields: 8-10 servings.

Vegetable Casserole

Elenna Firme
Gooseberry Patch Artisan

16 oz. poly bag of California blend style vegetables
    (broccoli, cauliflower, carrots)
1 can condensed cream of mushroom soup, undiluted
3 oz. cream cheese
1 c. shredded sharp
    cheddar cheese
1 c. corn flakes, crushed
4 oz. can sliced mushrooms
1/4 t. basil
1/4 t. celery salt
1/8 t. thyme
1 t. prepared mustard
1 T. margarine, melted

Prepare vegetables according to directions on package; drain. In a pan heat soup, cream cheese and cheddar cheese until sauce is smooth and cheese is melted. Combine vegetables and sauce, add mushrooms. Pour into a 1 1/2-quart casserole. Place corn flakes and spices in a plastic storage bag and crush with a rolling pin. Sprinkle crushed flakes on top of casserole and drizzle with melted margarine. Bake at 400 degrees for 15 minutes or until sauce bubbles. Makes 4-6 servings.

Bountiful Sides

Zucchini Casserole

Barb Agne
Gooseberry Patch

My family loves this so much and there are never any leftovers.

4 c. sliced zucchini	1 c. grated parmesan cheese
2 eggs, beaten well	1 T. butter or margarine
1 c. mayonnaise	1 c. crushed potato chips
1 chopped onion	or bread crumbs
1/4 c. green pepper, chopped	salt and pepper

Cook zucchini in 2 cups of boiling water or microwave until tender; drain. Mix eggs, mayonnaise, onion, green pepper, cheese and butter together; add the zucchini. Pour into a greased baking dish. Dab top with butter or margarine, then put crushed potato chips over the top. Bake at 350 degrees for 30 minutes.

Wild Rice Casserole

Mickey Johnson

1 to 1 1/4 c. wild rice, uncooked	1 lb. fresh sliced mushrooms
1 T. salt	(or 1 large can)
1/4 lb. butter	1/2 c. almonds, slivered
1 small onion, chopped fine	1 c. chicken broth

Soak rice overnight. Then cook rice in salted water, using the 1 tablespoon of salt, for 45-50 minutes. Drain and saute in butter, along with onion and mushrooms; until soft, but not brown. Mix cooked rice mixture, almonds, and chicken broth in a large casserole. Cover tightly and cook at 325 degrees for 1 hour. If it starts to dry out, add more broth. Sliced almonds may be used to decorate the top of the casserole. Casserole will keep and can be reheated.

Yummy Baked Apples

Leaving your apple intact, remove the core. An apple corer makes it easy. Stuff apple with nuts, raisins, brown sugar, pecans and a cinnamon stick. Bake in a slow oven for 30-40 minutes. Your house will smell wonderful!

✦Grand Harvest Buffet✦

Raisin-Cranberry Sauce

Laura Mastropaolo

A delicious glaze for your holiday ham or turkey!

2 1/4 c. golden raisins
2 c. orange juice
1 c. water
1/4 c. lemon juice
2/3 c. sugar
3 c. fresh or frozen cranberries
1 T. finely grated orange peel

Combine raisins, orange juice, water, lemon juice, and sugar in a 3-quart saucepan. Bring to a boil and stir until sugar dissolves. Reduce heat and simmer for 10 minutes. Add the cranberries and simmer 5 more minutes. Add orange peel and simmer another 5 minutes, until liquid barely covers solid ingredients; cool. Store in fridge for up to 1 month; freezer for a year.
Yields: 4 1/2 cups.

Chowders, Soups, Stews & Breads

Broccoli Cheese Soup

Tammy Moon

2 pkgs. frozen chopped broccoli, cooked and drained
1 lb. box pasteurized proccss cheese
    spread, cut into chunks
1 small onion, sliced thin
    (rings)
1 small can chicken broth
1 stick margarine
1/2 c. flour
2 c. milk

In a stock pot, saute onions in margarine, until onions are clear. Remove from heat; add flour, stir. (it will get smooth and thick). Add chicken broth and milk; cook until thick. Add cheese and broccoli; heat until cheese is melted. Serves 6.

Williamsburg Turkey Soup

Jan Kouzes

This is a hearty way to use the leftover turkey pieces following Thanksgiving or Christmas Dinner.

2 large onions, chopped
3 large celery stalks and
    leaves, chopped
2 large carrots, chopped
2 c. water
1/2 lb. butter
1 c. flour

2 1/2 qts. hot turkey or
    chicken broth
1 pt. half-and-half
1 c. diced cooked turkey
1 c. cooked rice
salt and pepper, to taste

In a medium saucepan over medium heat, cook onions, celery, and carrots in water; cover and cook 20 minutes. In a large saucepan, over low heat, melt the butter and stir in the flour, beating constantly. Then add broth and half-and-half; cook, stirring, until bubbly (4 to 5 minutes). Add the vegetables and their liquid and cook, stirring, for 10 minutes. Add the turkey and rice and season to taste. Serves 10-12.

> *O, it sets my heart a-clickin' like the tickin' of a clock,*
> *When the frost is on the punkin and the fodder's in the shock.*
> *James Whitcomb Riley*

Easy Velvet Broccoli Soup

Linda Day

10 oz. pkg. frozen broccoli,
   chopped or cuts
2 1/2 c. canned uncondensed
   chicken broth
1 bay leaf

1/4 c. chopped onion
2 egg yolks, beaten
1 t. butter
1 c. light cream or milk
salt and pepper

Bring to a boil in a saucepan broccoli, broth, bay leaf, and onion. Reduce heat, cover and simmer for 5 minutes, until broccoli is tender. Discard bay leaf. Put soup through a food mill or blender, or stir briskly with a wire whisk, for a few seconds. Drop beaten egg yolks and butter into whirling soup. Return to pan, stir in cream, salt and pepper. Serves 4.

Corn Chowder

Barbara Bargdill
Gooseberry Patch

I make this soup with the last picking of corn from the garden, but it's just as good with frozen corn!

1 medium onion, chopped
2 T. butter or margarine
2 c. diced potatoes
1 c. hot water
2 c. milk
2 T. flour
1 pkg. (10 oz.) frozen sweet
   whole kernel corn
1 t. salt
1/8 t. pepper

Saute onion in butter, in saucepan, until golden. Add potatoes and hot water. Bring to a boil. Cover, reduce heat; simmer until potatoes are tender. Gradually stir milk into flour. Add to potatoes along with corn, salt and pepper. Bring to a boil, reduce heat; stir occasionally; simmer about 10 minutes. Garnish with chopped parsley.

39

◆ Grand Harvest Buffet ◆

Clam Chowder
Cheryl Ewer

1 c. onions, finely chopped
1 c. celery, diced
2 c. potatoes, diced
2 cans (6 1/2 oz.) clams, drained
3/4 c. butter
3/4 c. flour

1 qt. (4 c.) half-and-half
1 1/2 t. salt
2 T. red wine vinegar
(optional)
dash of pepper

Pour clam juice over vegetables in small sauce pan. Add enough water to barely cover; simmer, covered, over medium heat until barely tender. In the meantime, melt butter; add flour and blend; cook. Add cream and stir with wire whip until smooth and thick. Add undrained vegetables, clams, and vinegar. Heat and season to taste.

Shrimp Chowder
Pat LaFlame

4 large onions, sliced thin
1/4 c. butter or margarine
1 c. boiling water
6 medium potatoes, pared
and cubed
1 T. salt

1/2 t. pepper
1 1/2 c. milk
2 c. (1/2 lb.) grated cheese
(cheddar, colby, etc.)
2 lbs. deveined shrimp

In a dutch oven, saute onions in butter or margarine. Add water, potatoes, salt and pepper; simmer, covered, for 20 minutes or until potatoes are tender. Meanwhile, heat milk and cheese until the cheese has melted (do not boil). To the potatoes and onions add the shrimp; cook until the shrimp turn pink (about 3 minutes). Add the hot milk/cheese mixture. Heat, again do not boil. Serve with a sprig of parsley. Makes 8 large servings.

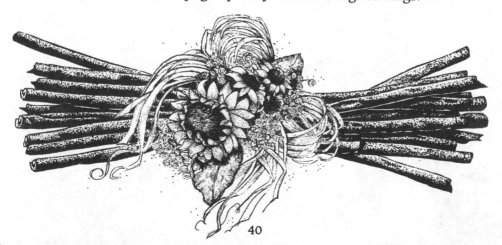

Sausage Soup

Janice Tobiaz

This is a wonderful, hearty soup. My husband cooks it for a meal and everyone leaves the table happy!

1 lb. sweet Italian sausage
1/2 c. chopped onion
1 can (16 oz.) stewed tomatoes

24 oz. beef broth
2 c. water
2 c. elbow macaroni

Remove sausage from casing. Brown sausage with onion in a large pan (6-8 quart) over medium heat. Drain fat. Stir in tomatoes, broth and water and bring to a boil. Reduce heat, cover and simmer for 15 minutes. Add macaroni and simmer for an additional 10 minutes or until macaroni is done. Makes 4 servings.

Cheddar Chowder

Sheri Berger

4 c. water
5 potatoes, cubed
4 carrots, cut up
1 onion, chopped
2 t. salt
1/2 t. pepper
1 bag frozen broccoli

1 stick margarine
1/2 c. flour
3 c. milk
3 c. cheddar cheese, shredded
3 c. ham, cubed

Combine water, salt, pepper and all vegetables, except broccoli. Bring water to a boil; boil until vegetables are soft. During the last 5 minutes of boiling, add the broccoli and cover the pot. In a separate pan, combine milk, flour and margarine, until melted. Add cheese and stir to melt. Add cheese mixture and ham to undrained vegetables. Heat, but don't boil. Serves 10-12.

Beef Barley Soup

Cathy Marcquenski

Serve with warm crusty bread and butter!

1 lb. boiling beef (labeled "beef for soup" in meat case)
2 qts. water
2 T. salt
parsley, snipped about 2 branches or 1 T. dried
2 leeks, diced

2 stalks celery, diced
3 to 4 medium carrots, diced
3/4 c. rice or 1/2 pkg. fine noodles
3/4 c. barley
2 or 3 potatoes, diced

In a large stove top kettle or soup pot place beef, water, salt, parsley, leeks, celery and carrots; cook until tender (dice beef if necessary). Then add rice or noodles, barley and potatoes. Keep simmering until cook time reaches about 4 hours or so. The longer it simmers the better, and thicker it gets. It's even better as a side dish leftover the next day. Yield: 8-10 servings, depending on how hungry your family is.

Hearty Vegetable Chowder

Robbi Courtaway

4 medium red potatoes, peeled and diced
2 medium carrots, sliced
1 stalk celery, chopped
1/2 medium onion, chopped
1 1/2 t. salt
1/2 t. pepper

2 c. boiling water
1/4 c. margarine
1/4 c. flour
2 c. milk
8 oz. pkg. shredded sharp cheddar cheese

In a 2-quart saucepan simmer vegetables, salt and pepper in water for 10 minutes; do not drain. While vegetables are cooking, melt margarine in another large, heavy saucepan or soup pot. Stir in flour and milk gradually to make a white sauce (use low heat). Add cheese and stir until melted. Add vegetables and water and heat thoroughly; do not boil. Serves 4-6. Recipe can be doubled.

This Thanksgiving, consider eating dinner at a restaurant, then returning home for a football game or a tree trimming party! If this seems too drastic of a change, this year you supply the house and have the others bring the dinner.

Tortilla Soup

Claire Pineda

whole chicken
celery
onion
salt
1 can tomatoes, cut up
1 can corn

2-3 T. chili powder
avocado
lime or lime juice
Monterey Jack cheese, grated
tortilla chips

Cook chicken in water to cover with celery, onion and salt; until tender. Strain broth, cut up chicken. Set chicken aside. With broth in pot, add tomatoes, corn and chili powder to taste; let simmer. Add chicken. Peel avocados, then cut up. Squeeze lime juice over avocado. To serve: In individual bowls, place a couple of pieces of avocado with lime juice, add broken tortilla chips, and grated Monterey Jack cheese. Pour soup over and top with cheese and chips. The amounts of everything can be varied...it doesn't have to be exact. Also, the lime juice makes a difference so do not leave out. Yields 6 to 8 servings.

Potato Tuna Chowder

Susan Harvey

2 1/2 c. diced potatoes
2 c. basic chicken stock
2 T. fresh minced onion
1/2 t. salt (optional)
1/4 t. sage
1/4 t. paprika

dash of white pepper
1/2 c. sliced fresh carrots
1/2 c. cut fresh green beans
1/2 c. sliced fresh celery
3 c. milk (or skim)
7 oz. can chunk style tuna

Combine 1 cup of potatoes, chicken stock, onion and salt in a large saucepan; bring to a boil. Reduce heat, cover; simmer 10-15 minutes, until potatoes are tender. Add sage, paprika, and pepper; mash potatoes. Add remaining potatoes, carrots, beans, celery and milk to potatoes; bring just to a boil. Reduce heat, simmer about 15 minutes until vegetables are tender. Break tuna into chunks, add to chowder. Simmer 5 minutes more. Yield: 4-6 servings.

•Grand Harvest Buffet•

The Great Pumpkin Stew

Eileen Curran

3 1/2 lbs. boneless beef, cut into cubes
3 T. vegetable oil
1 large onion, sliced
2 celery sticks with leaves,
    cut into small pieces
1 pt. canned (preserved)
    tomatoes; or 1 can (16 oz.)
    whole tomatoes
1 t. parsley
1/2 t. basil
1 t. salt
1/4 t. pepper
dash of celery salt
1 pumpkin about 10" to 12"
    in diameter
1 lb. (about 6 or 7) fresh
    carrots, peeled and sliced
6 medium potatoes, peeled
    and quartered

Heat oil in a heavy, large pot.
Add meat and brown on all
sides over medium heat. Add
sliced onion and celery and cook
until onion and celery are tender.
Add tomatoes and spices; cover and
simmer about 1 1/2 hours, or until meat
is almost tender. Prepare pumpkin while beef is simmering.
Cut off pumpkin top and reserve. Remove pumpkin seeds and membrane.
Scoop out pumpkin meat in chunks to measure 1 1/2 cups, being careful to
leave pumpkin wall about 1/2" thick (especially near the bottom). This way
the pumpkin shell will not collapse during cooking. Reserve pumpkin
chunks. After beef has simmered for approximately 1 1/2 hours, add sliced
carrots and let carrots cook about 10 minutes. Add peeled potato quarters,
cooking 15 to 20 minutes until potatoes are almost tender. Then stir pumpkin meat into beef mixture. Add more salt or pepper, if needed; bring to a
boil. If required, add small amount of water to mixture. Spoon stew into
pumpkin shell on a heavy baking pan and bake in a preheated 350 degree
oven about 1 1/2 hours, or until meat and vegetables are bubbling. Be
careful not to overcook as pumpkin shell may collapse. Serves 8.

Zucchini Sausage Soup

Alfreda Crosley

Very good with warm, crusty bread!

2 lbs. Italian sausage (sweet)
4 c. diced celery
4 medium onions, cut into strips

3 cans stewed tomatoes
  (15 oz. cans)
2 medium zucchini, sliced

Remove sausage from casings. Brown sausage in a deep soup pot. Add celery, and onion strips; saute until vegetables are tender. Add tomatoes and zucchini. Let simmer until zucchini is tender. Makes about 2 or 3 quarts.

10 Bean Soup

Rori Jensen

A hearty soup when the winter winds blow!
Mix together the following:

1 lb. baby lima beans
1 lb. pinto beans
1 lb. great northern beans
1 lb. split peas
1 lb. pearl barley
1 lb. black-eyed peas
1 lb. navy or kidney beans
1 lb. lentils
1 lb. pink beans
1 lb. black beans

Soak 2 cups of bean mix overnight.
Drain and add:

8 c. chicken broth or water
approximately 1 lb. ham
    hocks or ham shanks
1 large onion, diced
2 cloves garlic, crushed
16 oz. can stewed
    tomatoes

Cook 1 1/2 to 3 hours,
until beans are tender;
or all day in a crockpot.

Grand Harvest Buffet

Broccoli Crab Bisque

Karen Balistrieri

1 c. sliced leeks
1 c. sliced fresh mushrooms
1 c. fresh chopped broccoli
1 clove garlic, minced
1/4 c. butter or margarine
1/4 c. flour
1/4 t. dried thyme

1/8 t. pepper
1 small bay leaf
3 c. chicken broth
1 c. half-and-half
3 oz. shredded Swiss
    (low sodium may be used)
6 oz. crabmeat

In a 3-quart saucepan cook leeks, mushrooms, broccoli, and garlic in butter, until crisp-tender. Blend in flour, thyme, pepper and bay leaf. Add chicken broth and cream all at once. Cook and stir until thickened and bubbly. Add cheese; stir until melted. Add crab; heat through.

Old New England Cheddar Cheese Soup

Jan Kouzes

6 T. butter (divided in one half)
1 green pepper, seeded and diced
1 carrot, scraped and diced
1 onion, diced
1 stalk celery, diced
1/2 c. all-purpose flour
2 1/2 qt. warm milk
1 1/4 c. chicken broth
3/4 c. (3 oz.) shredded cheddar cheese
1 c. (4 oz.) shredded American cheese
    (or cubed pasteurized processed cheese spread)
1/4 c. dark beer or ale

Heat 3 of the tablespoons of butter in large saucepan and saute the green pepper, carrot, celery, and onion for about 10 minutes or until tender. Remove vegetables from the pot and set aside. In the same pot, heat the remaining 3 tablespoons of butter. Whisk in the flour and cook, whisking, until it foams and bubbles (2-3 minutes). Remove from heat and add the warm milk and broth, whisking briskly to blend. Return to heat and cook, stirring until smooth and thickened (10 minutes). Add the sauted vegetables and heat through. Reduce heat to very low and add the shredded cheeses, stirring with a fork until melted. Stir in the beer or ale and heat through. Taste for seasoning; the cheeses may be salty enough not to need any further seasoning. Serves 8-10.

No Knead Yeast Butter Rolls
Cheryl Neff

2 pkgs. yeast
1/2 c. lukewarm milk
1 lb. butter
2 c. cold milk

1/2 c. white sugar plus 2 T.
8 c. all-purpose flour
2 eggs, beaten
1 T. salt

Dissolve yeast with lukewarm milk and 2 tablespoons sugar. Melt butter in large bowl. Add cold milk, 1/2 cup sugar, salt, and eggs; mix well. Alternately add yeast and flour to the above mixture; mixing well after each addition. When mixed, leave dough in same bowl; cover and refrigerate at least 4 hours or overnight. On a lightly floured surface, divide dough into 4 parts. Roll each part separately into as large a circle as possible. Dough should be very thin. Cut into 16 wedges. Roll each piece from wide outside edge to center point. Lay point side down on ungreased baking sheet. Let rise in warm room until double in bulk (approximately 2-4 hours). Bake at 350 degrees for 15-20 minutes. Yield: 64 rolls.

Broccoli Corn Bread
Sylvia Crosby

1 box (8 1/2 oz.) corn muffin mix
1 box (10 oz.) chopped broccoli
4 eggs
1 c. cottage cheese

1 medium minced onion
1 stick margarine, melted
1 t. salt

Mix all ingredients in a large bowl. Bake at 400 degrees for 20-25 minutes in a 13"x9" pan.

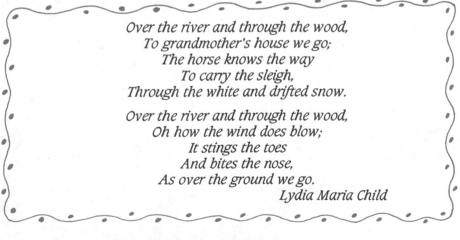

Over the river and through the wood,
To grandmother's house we go;
The horse knows the way
To carry the sleigh,
Through the white and drifted snow.

Over the river and through the wood,
Oh how the wind does blow;
It stings the toes
And bites the nose,
As over the ground we go.
Lydia Maria Child

◆ Grand Harvest Buffet ◆

Amy's Ap-peel-ing Apple Bread

Linda Zell

1/2 c. shortening
1 c. sugar
2 large eggs, beaten
1 t. vanilla
2 c. flour

1 t. baking soda
1/2 t. salt
2 T. buttermilk
2 c. peeled and diced apples

Preheat oven to 325 degrees. Cream shortening and sugar. Add eggs and vanilla; mix well. Add 1 cup of sifted dry ingredients; mix. Add buttermilk. Add last cup of dry ingredients. Fold in apples. Pour into a greased loaf pan (9"x5"x3"). Sprinkle on topping. Bake at 325 degrees for 45-60 minutes, until cake tester comes out clean. Cool in pan 15 minutes, then finish cooling on rack.

Topping:

2 T. soft margarine
1 t. cinnamon

2 T. flour
2 T. sugar

Mix until crumbly.

Butternut Rolls

Dawn Ross

4 c. flour
1 lb. butter or margarine
1/2 pt. sour cream
2 egg yolks

Mix together by hand until blended. Add a little more flour, if necessary, to prevent dough from sticking to sides of bowl (or your hands). Roll out dough a portion at a time. Cut into 8 equal pie shaped slices. Sprinkle filling on a slice and roll up. Place on cookie sheets and bake at 350 degrees for 30 minutes, or until lightly golden brown. Makes about 2 dozen.

Filling:

1 1/2 c. sugar
2 t. cinnamon
1 c. chopped walnuts

Stir until blended.

48

Cowboy Biscuits

Elenna Firme
Gooseberry Patch Artisan

7 c. flour
1 t. salt
1/2 t. baking soda
2 pkgs. yeast, dissolved
   in 1 c. warm water

1/2 c. sugar
4 full t. baking powder
2 c. buttermilk (you can use
   powdered mixed with water)
1/2 c. vegetable oil

Combine all ingredients and mix together well. Roll or pat a portion of dough on well floured surface to a thickness of 3/4". Cut with a large biscuit cutter or just break off pieces of dough and place on ungreased cookie sheet. Bake at 375 degrees for 10-12 minutes, or until done. Leftover dough can be stored in refrigerator up to 6 weeks, in an airtight container. Make sure there is extra room in the container, because the dough grows.

Beer Bread

Mariah Thompson

3 c. self-rising flour
1/3 c. sugar
16 oz. can of beer, room temperature
1 1/2 sticks of unsalted butter

Grease 8" to 10" cast iron skillet with 1/2 stick of unsalted butter and place in a 400 degree preheated oven for 6 to 7 minutes. In a large mixing bowl, whisk the flour and sugar together, add beer into bowl and whisk into a smooth batter. Pour batter into hot skillet and return to oven for 25 minutes. Melt the one stick of unsalted butter and pour over the entire top of the beer bread, when the 25 minutes are up. Place back into oven for an additional 20 minutes. Let stand about 10 minutes before cutting. This bread can be frozen.

Colonial Brown Bread

Kathy Bolyea

2 c. whole wheat flour
1/2 c. plus 3 T. flour
1 c. packed brown sugar

2 t. baking soda
2 c. buttermilk

Mix first 4 ingredients. Slowly add buttermilk. Mix until well blended. Pour into greased loaf pan. Bake at 350 degrees for 1 hour. Makes 1 loaf.

Star Croutons

Sara Walker

dense white bread
tiny star (or other shape) cookie cutter
2 T. butter
1 T. olive oil
minced or pressed garlic

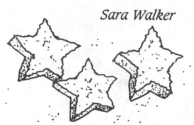

Cut out lots of stars (or other shape). In a skillet place butter, oil and garlic. Carefully toast cut-outs on each side. Cool and seal in a container. Adjust amount of butter and oil to the size of skillet and amount of bread cut-outs you are making; add more as needed.

Brad's "Great Pumpkin" Bread

Joanne Martin-Robinson
Gooseberry Patch

Especially good on Halloween night!

3 c. all-purpose flour
2 c. sugar
2 t. baking soda
1 t. ground cloves
1 t. cinnamon
1 t. nutmeg

1 t. salt
1/2 t. double-acting baking powder
16 oz. can (2 c.) pumpkin
2/3 c. salad oil
3 eggs, slightly beaten

Preheat oven to 350 degrees. Grease two standard loaf pans. Mix the flour, sugar, baking soda, cloves, cinnamon, nutmeg, salt and baking powder in a large bowl, using a fork to mix. Add the remaining ingredients and mix until well blended. Pour into the loaf pans. Bake about 1 hour or until toothpick inserted in center comes out clean. Cool on wire racks for 10 minutes or so before removing from pans and cooling completely. Best if made a day ahead.

Apple Snow

3 large cooking apples   white of one egg
6 T. powdered sugar

Wash and dry three apples; prick them in a few places, and bake in moderate oven (350 degrees) until soft. Remove the skin, and run the pulp through a sieve. Beat the egg white to a froth; add sugar gradually; then add apple pulp and beat it all together until thoroughly mixed, light and soft.

Old-Fashioned Sweets

Apple Cider

✦ Grand Harvest Buffet ✦

Grape Pie

Loretta Nichols
(Vickie's Mom)

We have grown grapes in our backyard grape arbor for the past 35 years. Full of old-fashioned goodness, there's nothing like a slice of grape pie in the fall!

2 lbs. Concord grapes	1/8 t. salt
3/4 c. sugar	1 T. lemon juice
1/4 c. flour	pastry for 8" double crust

Wash grapes thoroughly, then stem (there should be 4 cups stemmed grapes). Press the clear pulp from the skins, saving the skins in a bowl and letting the pulp and juice drop into a saucepan. Cook the pulp over low heat for 5 minutes; then turn into a strainer or food mill and press the pulp through into the bowl containing the skins; discard the seeds. Mix sugar, flour and salt, and add to grapes. Stir in lemon juice. Pour cooled mixture into pastry-lined pie pan. Roll out pastry for upper crust. Cut a design for steam vents. Moisten rim with cold water. Lay pastry over pie, press to seal edge, trim, turn under. Let rest 10 minutes and flute edge. Bake in hot oven (450 degrees) for 15 minutes; reduce heat to 325 degrees (moderately slow) and bake 30 minutes longer until the crust is golden brown. Cool 3 or 4 hours on cake rack before cutting.

Popcorn Balls

Jennifer Overfield

Mom and Dad ran a popcorn farm and all of us kids helped, from planting to harvest. Making this treat was a wonderful finish to a good harvest.

2/3 c. white syrup	1/8 t. baking soda
2 T. vinegar	2 t. cream of tartar
2 T. butter	1 popper of popped
2 c. sugar	corn, unsalted
2 t. vanilla	
2/3 c. boiling water	

Combine syrup, sugar and vinegar in the boiling water. When mixture boils, add cream of tartar. Boil to soft crack stage and add butter, soda and vanilla. For color add food coloring to desired shade. Pour over popped corn and stir well. Butter hands well (keep extra butter on hand), then form popcorn balls. Set on waxed paper.

Pumpkin Ribbon Bread
Gail Allen

This bread is beautiful when cut, with the slices fanned out on a serving plate.

Filling:
2 pkgs. (3 oz. each) cream
   cheese, softened
1/3 c. sugar
1 T. flour
1 egg
2 t. grated orange peel

Bread:
1 c. cooked pumpkin
1/2 c. vegetable oil
2 eggs
1 1/2 c. sugar
1/2 t. salt
1/2 t. cloves
1/2 t. cinnamon
1 2/3 c. all-purpose flour
1 t. baking soda
1 c. chopped pecans

For filling, beat cream cheese, sugar and flour together in a small bowl. Add egg; mix to blend. Stir in orange peel; set aside. Make bread by combining pumpkin, oil and eggs in a large bowl. Add sugar, salt, cloves, cinnamon, flour, baking soda, and pecans; mix to blend. Pour 1/4 of batter into 2 greased and floured 7 1/2"x3 1/3"x3" loaf pans. Carefully spread the cream cheese mixture over batter. Add remaining batter, covering filling. Bake at 325 degrees for 1 1/2 hours, or until bread tests done with wooden pick. Cool for 10 minutes before removing from pans. Store in refrigerator. Makes 2 loaves.

Apple Nut Dessert Cake
Patty Kuehn

1/4 c. butter, softened
1 c. white sugar
1 egg
1/2 c. chopped walnuts (optional)
3 large apples, peeled and chopped

1/2 t. salt
1/2 t. cinnamon
1 c. flour
1 t. baking soda

Stir together all ingredients and put into a well greased 8"x9" pan. Bake at 350 degrees for 35 minutes. While baking, stir the following ingredients in a medium saucepan and cook over low heat, stirring occasionally.

Sauce:

1/2 c. butter
1 t. flour
1/2 c. cream

1 t. vanilla
1 c. brown sugar, packed

Serve over hot cake.

Grand Harvest Buffet

Apple Grunt

Cathy Marcquenski

3 T. butter
1/2 c. sugar
1 egg
1 1/4 c. flour
1/2 t. baking soda
1 t. baking powder
1/2 t. salt
1/2 c. buttermilk
2 1/4 c. pared, diced apples

Brown Sugar Topping:

1/3 c. brown sugar
1 T. flour
1/2 t. cinnamon
2 T. butter, softened

Preheat oven to 425 degrees. Cream together the butter and sugar. Beat in the egg. Sift together the flour, soda, baking powder and salt. Add to the creamed mixture alternately with the buttermilk. Stir in the apples. Pour into an 8"x8" baking dish or pan. Mix topping ingredients together until crumbly. Sprinkle over top of apple mixture. Bake for 30 minutes. Serves 6 to 8.

Caramel Apple Salad

Toni Tobin

A great side dish with turkey!

1 small package instant butterscotch pudding
8 oz. carton frozen whipped topping, thawed
8 oz. can crushed pineapple with juice
1 c. mini marshmallows
3 c. chopped apples, with peelings
1 c. dry roasted peanuts (optional)

In a large bowl, mix together the dry pudding, whipped topping, pineapple and juice until well blended. Stir in the apples, marshmallows and peanuts until thoroughly mixed. Refrigerate 1-2 hours before serving. Serves 8.

Grandma Mac's Banana Cake
With Brown Sugar Frosting

Juanita Williams

Great old-fashioned recipe!

1/2 c. butter
1 c. bananas, mashed
1 t. baking powder
1/2 t. baking soda
3 eggs

1 1/2 c. sugar
1 3/4 c. flour, sifted
4 T. sour milk
1 c. walnuts, chopped

Cream together butter and sugar; add mashed ripe bananas. Sift together flour and baking powder; add to banana mixture. Add sour milk, baking soda and chopped walnuts. Beat well. Add one egg at a time, beating between eggs. Bake in shallow 13"x9" loaf pan, at 350 degrees for approximately 30-35 minutes.

Brown Sugar Frosting:

5 T. brown sugar
2 T. butter
1 c. powdered sugar

2 T. milk
1 t. vanilla

Melt brown sugar with milk and butter; boil for 1 minute. Let cool; then beat until creamy, adding vanilla and enough powdered sugar until easily spreadable. Frost cake when cool.

Grama's Apple Crisp

Kathleen Popp

Serve warm with vanilla ice cream. Yummy!

8-10 apples, peeled, cored
    and sliced
3/4 c. sugar
1 T. cinnamon
1 c. flour
1 c. sugar

1/4 t. salt
1 t. baking powder
1 egg
6 T. butter
vanilla ice cream
nuts, if desired

Fill a large glass 13"x9"x2" baking dish three-fourths full of sliced apples. Cover with sugar and cinnamon on top, adding nuts if desired. Let stand while you mix together the flour, sugar, salt and baking powder. Beat egg until light and work into flour mixture until crumbly. Take this by the handfuls and crumble over apples. Melt butter and pour over the top. Bake at 350 degrees for 45 minutes, until crust is lightly browned. Yield: 16 servings.

Fall Pumpkin Squares

Barb McFaden

2 t. cinnamon
1 t. baking soda
1 t. salt
1 t. vanilla
4 eggs

2 c. sugar
2 c. flour
2 c. pumpkin
1 c. oil

Mix all ingredients together. I use a jelly pan, but a 13"x9" pan is fine too. Pour mixture into pan and bake at 350 degrees for 20-30 minutes (until toothpick comes out clean).

Icing:

2 to 2 3/4 c. powdered sugar
8 to 11 oz. cream cheese

3/4 stick butter
2 t. vanilla

Mix all ingredients in a bowl. Spread on cooled pumpkin squares. Keep refrigerated.

Raisin Apple Harvest Cake

Judy Borecky

3 c. diced apples
3 c. flour
2 1/2 c. sugar
1 1/4 c. oil
4 large eggs
1 T. plus 1 t. vanilla extract
2 t. cinnamon

1 1/2 t. salt
1 1/2 t. baking soda
1/2 t. cloves
1/2 t. baking powder
2/3 c. or 1 c. raisins
1 c. chopped walnuts

Place all ingredients (except the apples, raisins and nuts) in a large bowl. Using mixer, beat until well blended. Stir in apples, raisins and nuts. Pour into 2 sprayed loaf (bread) pans. Bake at 325 degrees for 1 hour or until done. Test with a toothpick. May be frosted with Cream Cheese Frosting.

Cream Cheese Frosting:

1/4 c. margarine, softened
4 oz. cream cheese, softened
1 t. vanilla
2 c. powdered sugar

Mix all ingredients well. Frost cake. Also great for carrot cake.

Old Timey Apple Brownies

Dora Poythress

1 stick melted butter or
    margarine
2 eggs
1 c. white sugar

1 c. brown sugar
2 c. self-rising flour
2 c. chopped peeled apples
2 t. cinnamon

Mix all ingredients together. Pour into a greased brownie pan. Bake at 350 degrees for about 30 minutes.

Mom's Carrot Cake

Debbie Kephart

The crushed pineapple gives this cake a moistness you can't resist!

2 c. sugar
2 c. flour
2 t. baking soda
1 t. salt
3 t. cinnamon
16 oz. can crushed pineapple
    (drained)

1 1/2 c. vegetable oil
4 eggs
3 c. grated carrots
1/2 c. chopped pecans

Preheat oven at 350 degrees. Grease and flour a 11"x9" cake pan. Mix sugar, flour, baking soda, salt and cinnamon in small bowl. Set aside. Mix oil, eggs, pineapple and carrots. Beat in dry ingredients. Fold in pecans. Pour into pan and bake 30-35 minutes, or until center is done. Frost with frosting when cool.

Frosting:

1 stick butter
1 (8 oz.) block cream
    cheese
1 box powdered sugar
2 t. vanilla extract
1/2 c. pecans

Beat butter and cream
cheese until smooth.
Blend in powdered
sugar and vanilla.
Fold in pecans.

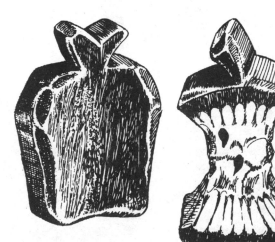

Grand Harvest Buffet

Pumpkin Layered Dessert

Judy Borecky

A taste of heaven!

Crust:

1 c. flour	1/2 c. margarine, softened
2 T. sugar	1/2 c. chopped walnuts

Mix together ingredients and pat into a 13"x9" pan or pyrex. Bake at 350 degrees about 15 minutes, until golden. Let cool.

2nd Layer:

8 oz. package cream cheese, softened
1 c. powdered sugar
one-half of a 12 oz. tub frozen whipped topping, thawed

Beat cream cheese and sugar well. Stir in whipped topping and spread on cooled crust.

3rd Layer:

16 oz. can pumpkin	1 t. cinnamon
2 small pkgs. vanilla	1/2 t. powdered ginger
instant pudding mix	1/4 t. cloves
1 c. half-and-half	

Beat and spread over cream cheese layer. Chill for 1 hour. Serve with a dollop of frozen whipped topping and a sprinkle of chopped walnuts.

Caramel Corn

Deborah Donovan

2 qts. popped corn
1 1/3 c. sugar
1 c. butter (do not use margarine)
1 t. vanilla
1/2 c. white corn syrup

Combine sugar, syrup and butter. Bring to a boil over medium heat; stir constantly (do not let burn), about 6-7 minutes. It will make a soft caramel. Remove from heat, add vanilla and spread over popped corn. Stir thoroughly with spatula. Cool. Eat and enjoy.

Old-Fashioned Sweets

Not-So-Sweet Pecan Pie

Judy Borecky

My mom has had this recipe since the early 1930's. She still makes it and she is 85!

3/4 c. white sugar
3/4 c. white corn syrup
2 t. vanilla
3 eggs, beaten

1/8 t. salt
1 T. flour
3 T. margarine, melted
2 c. slightly broken pecans

Mix all ingredients except the eggs. Beat the eggs and add to mixture. Pour into an unbaked pie crust (9") and bake at 300 degrees for 40 minutes, then turn oven up to 350 degrees and bake for an additional 15-20 minutes. I sometimes put in 1/2 cup of chocolate chips for a different, yummy flavor.

Crust:

1 c. flour
1/2 t. salt

1/3 c. vegetable shortening
3 T. cold water

Using pastry cutter, blend flour, salt and shortening. Stir in water and roll out crust.

Pecan Fingers

Jane Keichinger

1 c. butter
1/2 c. powdered sugar
2 t. vanilla

2 c. flour
2 c. pecans, finely chopped

Cream butter. Mix in vanilla, powdered sugar and flour. Add pecans, mixing well. Chill dough. Roll into finger lengths and place on a greased cookie sheet. Bake at 250 degrees for 1 hour. Roll in powdered sugar while still warm. These freeze well.

Apple Butter

4 qts. apples
2 qts. water
1 1/2 qts. cider
1 1/2 lbs. sugar

1 t. cinnamon
1 t. allspice
1 t. cloves

Wash apples and slice into small bits. Cover with water and boil until soft. Press through a sieve to remove skins and seeds. Bring cider to a boil, add apple pulp and sugar and cook until thickened, stirring constantly to prevent scorching. Add spices and cook 20 minutes more. Fill 3 sterilized quart jars and seal.

◆ Grand Harvest Buffet ◆

Gingerbread

Gail Hageman

1 egg, well beaten
1/2 c. sugar
1/2 c. dark molasses
1/4 c. butter
1/2 c. hot water
1 T. grated orange rind

2 c. cake flour, sifted
1/4 t. salt
1 t. ginger
1 t. cinnamon
1 t. baking soda

Combine and beat well the egg, sugar and molasses. Mix butter into hot water and stir until melted. Add butter mixture to sugar, egg and molasses. Sift the dry ingredients together and add to other mixture. Pour into a lightly greased bundt mold. Bake at 350 degrees for about 30 minutes. Unmold when cooled and dust with powdered sugar. Serves 8-10.

The Best Apple Walnut Raisin Pie

Joanne A. Jacobellis

10" pie crust
3 tart red apples, peeled and
   thinly sliced
1 1/4 c. water
3/4 c. plus 2 T. sugar
2 T. cornstarch
3/4 c. graham cracker crumbs
1/2 c. (1 stick) butter, room
   temperature

6 to 8 T. dark raisins
1/4 c. chopped walnuts
1 T. fresh lemon juice
1/4 t. vanilla
pinch each of: cinnamon,
   mace & nutmeg

Arrange apples over crust. Place rack in middle of oven and preheat to 400 degrees. Combine 1 cup of water and 3/4 cup sugar in small sauce pan; bring to a boil over medium heat, stirring until sugar dissolves; then boil 10 minutes more without stirring. Add cornstarch dissolved in remaining water, and stir constantly until thickened. Pour over apples. Thoroughly combine crumbs, butter, raisins and walnuts. Mix in remaining ingredients and sprinkle evenly over apples. Bake 15 minutes; cover with foil, and bake 30 minutes longer. Serve warm.

> *Here's a way to make a regular pumpkin pie into something special!*
> *With pie dough scraps, cut out eyes, nose and mouth*
> *and place on top of pie to resemble a jack-o'-lantern.*
> *Bake as directed.*

Pennsylvania Dutch Apple Muffin Cake

Gail Hageman

This can be made ahead of time and frozen. Thaw and warm it a bit before serving. I like to serve this for breakfast when we have overnight guests.

2 c. flour	1/4 t. cloves
1 T. baking powder	1 1/4 c. sugar
1/2 t. baking soda	1/4 c. butter
1 t. salt	2 eggs
1 1/4 t. cinnamon	1 c. sour cream
1/2 t. allspice	1 c. finely diced, peeled apples

Heat oven to 350 degrees. Butter an 8 cup souffle dish and coat bottom and sides with bread crumbs, tapping out excess. A 9" tube pan may also be used. Combine dry ingredients, blending well. Melt butter in pan, remove from heat and stir in sour cream. Then beat in the eggs. Beat the butter mixture into the dry mixture and blend until batter is smooth and satiny. Stir in apple. Pour batter into prepared pan and level. Sprinkle with crumb topping. Bake for 1 hour until crumbs are crisp and lightly browned. If tube pan is used, test for doneness after 45 minutes. Cool cake in pan 20 minutes. Run a knife between cake and sides of pan and gently invert cake onto counter. Re-invert on a rack and cool thoroughly.

Crumb Topping:

1/4 c. sugar	1/4 t. cinnamon
3 T. flour	2 T. cold butter

In a bowl blend the sugar, flour and cinnamon. Cut in cold butter until mixture forms coarse crumbs. Serves 8-10.

Caramel Apple Slice Dip

Peg Buckingham
Gooseberry Patch

1 pkg. caramels
8 oz. pkg. cream cheese

Combine caramels and cream cheese. Microwave until warm and creamy; stirring several times during warming. Serve as a dip with fresh, unpeeled apple slices spritzed with lemon juice so they stay snowy white.

Grand Harvest Buffet

Pumpkin Ice Cream Pie
Brenda Umphress

9" graham cracker crust
1/2 gal. vanilla ice cream
1 c. pumpkin
1/2 c. brown sugar

1/2 t. ginger
1/4 t. cinnamon
1/4 t. nutmeg
1 T. orange juice

Place ice cream in a large bowl, cut it up and allow to soften. Mix pumpkin with the other ingredients using an electric mixer. Add to the softened ice cream and mix well. Heap into cooled graham cracker crust. Freeze. Garnish each serving with a dollop of whipped cream. Serves 8.

Grandma Liz's Pumpkin Pie
Susan Kirschenheiter

This was my mother-in-law's recipe. It is not an "orange" colored pie, but very dark and rich because of all the spices. I don't eat "orange" pumpkin pies anymore!

1 1/4 c. cooked and strained pumpkin (canned is fine)
1/2 c. brown sugar, packed
1 T. cooking oil
1/4 t. each: ginger, nutmeg and cloves
2 eggs
1/2 t. each: cinnamon, allspice and salt
1 1/4 c. scalded milk, cooled and strained

Scald milk and when it has cooled to warm, stir in the brown sugar. In a bowl, mix oil, spices and salt with the pumpkin; then add the eggs; then add the milk/brown sugar mixture, mixing thoroughly. Pour mixture into a pie crust and bake 50-60 minutes in a 350 degree oven (pre-bake crust a bit for dryness). Check center of pie to make sure it is done. When making two pies, use 5 eggs.

Pecan Cheesecake

Judy Borecky

8 oz. cream cheese, softened
1/3 c. sugar
1 t. vanilla

1 large egg
1 1/4 c. chopped pecans

Whisk together the cream cheese, sugar, vanilla and egg until smooth. Pour into a 10" unbaked pastry crust. Sprinkle chopped pecans over filling. In another bowl, place:

3 large eggs
1 c. white corn syrup

1 t. vanilla
1/2 c. sugar

Whisk until smooth. Pour mixture over pecans. Bake at 350 degrees for 50-60 minutes until pastry is set and golden. Let cool. Pecans will rise to the top of the cheesecake and will have a layered appearance when cut.

Raisin Spice Bars

Eleanor R. Moore

2 c. sugar
2 c. water
2 c. raisins
1 c. butter

2 t. ground cloves
1 t. salt
3 1/2 c. sifted flour
1 t. baking soda

Combine sugar, water, raisins, butter, cloves and salt; bring to a boil, stirring occasionally. Boil for 1 minute, then remove from heat. Mix in flour and baking soda (dissolved in 1 tablespoon of water). Spread into lightly buttered 11 1/2"x17 1/2" pan. Bake at 350 degrees for 15 minutes or until middle puffs slightly. Cool, frost, cut into bars.

Frosting:

1 1/2 c. powdered sugar
1/4 t. vanilla
2 to 3 T. milk

Combine and beat until smooth; adding enough liquid to make icing easy to spread thinly over bars.

Grand Harvest Buffet

Pumpkin Cookies with Caramel Frosting

Denise Krasucki

1 c. margarine
1 c. sugar
1 t. vanilla
1 c. canned pumpkin
2 eggs
pinch of salt

2 c. flour
1 t. cinnamon
1 t. baking powder
1 t. baking soda
1 c. chopped walnuts
1 box raisins

Cream margarine, sugar, vanilla, pumpkin, eggs and salt. Sift flour, cinnamon, baking soda and baking powder; add to creamed mixture. Add walnuts and raisins; mixing well. Bake at 350 degrees for 15-20 minutes on an ungreased cookie sheet. Frost with caramel frosting.

Caramel Frosting:

3 T. butter
4 T. milk
1/2 c. brown sugar (dark),
   firmly packed

1 c. powdered sugar, sifted
3/4 t. vanilla

Combine butter, milk and brown sugar in a saucepan. Boil for 2 minutes, stirring constantly. Cool. Stir in sugar and vanilla. Beat until smooth and creamy.

Applesauce Raisin Drops

Marlene Wetzel-Dellagatta

1 c. packed brown sugar
3/4 c. shortening
1/2 c. applesauce
1 egg
2 1/4 c. all-purpose flour
3/4 t. ground cinnamon

1/2 t. baking soda
1/2 t. salt
1/4 t. ground cloves
1 c. raisins
1/2 c. chopped walnuts

Preheat oven to 375 degrees. Mix together brown sugar, shortening, applesauce and egg. Stir in remaining ingredients. Drop by rounded teaspoonsful about 2" apart onto ungreased cookie sheet. Bake 11-12 minutes. Makes about 5 dozen.

> *What calls back the past, like the rich pumpkin pie?*
> *John Greenleaf Whittier*

Old-Fashioned Sweets

Mom Schantz's Walnut Pumpkin Pudding

Phyllis Ann Schantz

1 c. walnuts, chopped
1/2 c. butter
1 c. brown sugar, packed
1/4 c. granulated sugar
1/2 t. each cinnamon,
   nutmeg and ginger
2 eggs well beaten

2 c. sifted all-purpose flour
1 1/2 t. baking powder
1/4 t. baking soda
1 1/2 t. salt
1 c. canned pumpkin
1/2 c. sour cream

Cream butter, brown sugar, white sugar and spices until fluffy. Beat in eggs and stir in nuts. Re-sift flour with baking powder, soda and salt. Add to creamed mixture alternately with pumpkin and sour cream. Turn into a well greased 1 1/2 to 2-quart mold; cover tightly. Set mold in a pan of hot water. Water should come halfway up the sides of the mold; replenish if necessary during steaming. Cover pan and steam pudding in continuous boiling water for 2 hours. Serve hot with Brandy Whipped Cream Sauce.

Brandy Whipped Cream Sauce:

1 egg
1/3 c. melted butter
1 1/2 c. sifted powdered sugar

pinch of salt
1 T. brandy extract
1 c. whipping cream

Beat egg. Beat in the butter, sugar, salt and brandy extract; set aside. Next, beat whipping cream until stiff. Gently fold cream into the butter mixture. Cover and chill until ready to serve. Serve over warm pudding.

Indian Pudding

1 qt. milk, plus 1 c.
6 T. corn meal moistened with a bit of cold milk
1 beaten egg
3/4 c. molasses
1 c. sugar
Lump of butter the size of an egg
1 t. each of ginger, cinnamon and salt

Scald 1 quart milk and add corn meal. Add egg and cook on low heat until very thick. Add rest of ingredients and pour into buttered baking dish. Pour a cup of cold milk over all. Bake 3 hours at 300 degrees. Remove milk scum and beat pudding until smooth with fork. Serve warm with whipped cream.

Cranberry Dessert

Deborah Lyddon

1 1/2 t. melted butter
1/2 c. sugar
1 c. flour
1/2 c. evaporated milk
1 1/2 t. baking powder
1/2 t. salt
2 c. washed fresh cranberries, uncooked

Mix well and place in 6 greased custard cups or 8 muffin cup pan. Bake at 350 degrees for 30 minutes.

Sauce:

1 stick butter
1 t. vanilla
1 c. sugar
1/2 c. evaporated milk

Melt butter; add other ingredients. Boil for 3 to 4 minutes. Keep warm over hot water. Serve cranberry muffin covered with sauce in small dessert bowls. Keep extra sauce handy for those who want more. Makes 6 if using custard cups; or 8 muffins.

Apple Cider Cake

1 1/2 sticks margarine
2 c. sugar
2 eggs
1 c. apple cider
1 t. baking soda
1 1/2 t. salt
2 t. cinnamon
3 c. flour
1 c. English walnuts
chopped dates or raisins
can also be used

Cream margarine, sugar and eggs. Stir soda into cider and add to mixture. Sift flour, salt and cinnamon and add gradually to mixture, beating after each addition. Add nuts. Pour cake batter into an angel food cake pan which has been greased and floured.
Bake at 375 degrees for about 40 minutes, then reduce heat to 325 degrees and bake about 15 minutes longer. Cake is done when toothpick inserted in center of cake comes out clean.

Celebration of Christmas

"You merry folk, be of good cheer,
For Christmas comes but once a year.
From open door you'll take no harm
By winter if your hearts are warm."
Geoffrey Smith

A Cozy Country Christmas

Try flavoring your whipped cream with such things as mixing in a little instant coffee, liqueurs, or flavored extracts such as almond, vanilla or peppermint. Top your favorite drinks (hot chocolate, eggnog, coffees) with these. Experiment with different flavors...use your imagination!

Janey Schultz

A very lovely Christmas sharing idea for a group of children is to make a "Mitten Christmas Tree" from cardboard and attach it to a wall. Each child in the group is asked to bring in a pair of mittens from home (newly purchased) and decorate the tree. Before Christmas arrives, the mittens are taken down by the children and delivered to a specific shelter for children and adults. The children take great pleasure seeing their decorations are going to help so many people, who might experience cold hands and fingers during the upcoming months.

To give a warm welcome to guests as they arrive at your home, play Beethoven, Mozart, Nutcracker Suite, etc., very softly in the background.

Jan Kouzes

For a special sparkle at your holiday table, light a white candle in a clear glass votive holder and put one at each placesetting. Don't worry about having all the votive cups match. Each one in my collection is different. When I use them all together on the table, the effect is lovely.

Holiday parties and dinners can be difficult for people on restricted diets. Help make holiday occasions even happier by preparing some foods you know your allergic, diabetic, or diet-restricted friends and family members will be able to eat.

Chris Murphy

During the holidays, I often take cake, cookies or breads to potlucks and parties. To avoid the hassles of returning dishes, I buy large dinner plates at rummage sales for $1.00 or less. Just let the hostess know that she doesn't have to return the plate and to pass it on when she goes to a party. These dishes are much sturdier than paper plates and prettier than aluminum pans. A holiday doily can be used to cover up a plate with a design.

Carol Suehiro

I like to give homemade gifts to friends and family. One of my favorite things to do is buy an inexpensive basket and fill it with inexpensive little things. I like to create a theme for each basket. If someone likes to write, I'll use stationery, note cards, pencils and a book of stamps; another favorite is a bath basket with sponges, decorative soaps, pretty washcloths, lotion and bath beads. I like to give goodie baskets too. I'll make a couple of batches of cookies and, knowing that a lot of people are health conscious now, I'll bake some type of banana bread or cake in mini loaf pans or muffin tins. I divide the cookies into batches of 4 or 5 and also divide one large cheese ball into 4 or 5 mini cheeseballs. I'll place all these goodies in a basket and tie with a big bow or place them in a pretty gift bag (Christmas, of course). This gives a sample of everything, without a lot of waste. They make nice hostess gifts. I've also added a "homemade" potpourri which I make by purchasing a large bag of holiday potpourri and dividing it into 4 small clear plastic bags, tying a pretty ribbon at the top. By putting so many different things together, it looks like more thought was put into it than one larger gift.

Lori Stricklen

I collect old canning jars from flea markets and garage sales. I fill them with my own homemade potpourri, but you could use purchased potpourri. Place a lace or crocheted doily around the open top of a jar and lace some ribbon through the openings. The scent of the potpourri fills a room.

Jeanne Elmer

One of my favorite ways to wrap all my special gifts is to use red or green check tissue paper, raffia for the bow, and tie on a small star or heart made from a cinnamon applesauce mix (vanilla is a nice change too!). This way the person can keep a part of the gift and use it on the tree next year. My children love to "help" make some of these ornaments for a tree they decorate and keep in their bedroom.

Anne McKinney
Gooseberry Patch Artisan

A Cozy Country Christmas

Put your talent to good use this Christmas and have a "Crafters Exchange Party." It works like this, invite eight to twelve creative people over to your home for the afternoon. Each person invited has to bring eight to twelve handmade gifts, depending, of course, upon the attendance. They can make food items, crafts that involve sewing, holiday ornaments, wood items, whatever their particular talent may be. When all your talented guests show up, have them put the presents, with everyone's names on them, under the tree. Serve refreshments, exchange the gifts and have fun! Everyone should end up with eight or twelve different handmade presents. This is a great way to share craft ideas or recipes and to feel proud that these special gifts were handcrafted for you.

Let's not forget about the senior citizens in our community this holiday season. Round up your adorable feline and your loyal canine, call your friends and ask to borrow their pets and head down to your local retirement home. Be sure to call the staff at the facility and make prior arrangements first. Animals have been known to lower people's blood pressure and they are wonderful companions. The senior citizens will enjoy an afternoon with these loving pets and you will be helping to provide some companionship for the elderly. Don't forget the senior citizen that lives alone who may want a pet as a more permanent companion. You can play "matchmaker" for the day and take that person to a local animal shelter, as they have many adorable pets that desperately need good homes.

Michelle Gardner

Fill a grapevine basket (with handle) with a crock filled with herb butter, a homemade loaf of garlic bread and an antique butter knife. Wrap with cellophane and tie off with a big homespun bow with a sprig of evergreen tucked in. Great for a boss, teacher and special neighbors!

Tina Main

For elderly or shut-ins buy boxes of greeting cards...include anniversary, birthday, sympathy, etc. Wrap them along with a book of stamps. They love having a card on hand instead of asking someone to make a special trip for them.

Kathy Deneault

If you're short on space, but have plenty of little paper treasures stored away, as I do, make a Christmas or Halloween display under a glass-topped table. Remove glass and clean. Underneath, add old cards, postcards, an old doily or fabric scraps, flat buttons or flat-backed rhinestones, old calling cards, tickets or other memorabilia...whatever looks good. Arrange to your liking and replace glass top, placing four foam or felt pads underneath at corners, if necessary, to raise the height of the glass. If you don't have a glass-topped table, you can have a piece of 1/4" thick beveled-edged glass cut (you can get this done fairly incxpensively at any window glass or auto glass shop) to fit your favorite table. It's fun to change the arrangements seasonally for Halloween, Thanksgiving, Christmas, Valentine's Day, Easter, July 4th, and general summer/winter displays. Old postcards and memorabilia can be found inexpensively at flea markets and garage sales. During the "off season" these treasures can be stashed in a shoe or sweater box and stored in a closet. Collecting new ones throughout the year can become addictive!

Robbi Courtaway

Prune your evergreen shrubs and trees and use for wreaths, centerpieces and roping. Tuck sprays of greens around pictures, on the table, over the doors and into the hands of all who come into your home.

Elizabeth Phillips

"Tis the season for cold winter noses, cheeks red as roses and warm, happy hearts.

Tessa Adelman

Make sugared fruit by dipping apples, grapes, pears and plums in egg white, then in white sugar. They look very pretty and frosty when placed in a pretty bowl with some greenery tucked in. Place the bowl on a lace doily.

Put a ribbon and/or a bell on your dog or cat on Christmas Day.

Give candy and cookies in old crockery bowls, fabric covered boxes, stencilled brown paper bags or baskets lined with a pretty new dish towels.

Sara Walker

A Cozy Country Christmas

I bake holiday breads in various sizes of tin cans. The bread can be baked and then frozen right in the can for several months before the holidays. Thaw before giving, wrap or have your children decorate the cans. Cookies can also be baked, stored in coffee cans and frozen. All you will have to do is decorate or wrap the can for a lovely gift.

Mickey Johnson

If you are invited to a bridal or baby shower in November or December, include a Christmas ornament with your gift.

Sandy Kolb

Little mittens that have been outgrown look precious hanging on the Christmas tree.

Brenda Umphress

If you have never made greenery wreaths before, it's something you should try. My husband and I have been making them since our first Christmas. We go into the woods one week before Thanksgiving and fill two large burlap bags full of greens. (Leave them outside in the cold to keep them fresh and green.) After Thanksgiving, the fun of making the wreaths begins! Tie bunches of greens onto a wire wreath, that can be purchased at a craft store. Keep following the outside circle, then do the inside circle. Place a hook on the back and a big red bow on the front. I have fun decorating the outside of my house with the wreaths. It gives the house a real old-fashioned country Christmas look.

Jackie Bankovic

I use old (antique) single jello molds in holiday shapes, filling them half full with salt, then placing a votive candle in them. I use them around the house during the holiday season for candlelight.

Tammy Anundson

Take a walk in the woods and collect pinecones, moss, pine, evergreen, nuts and pods and fill a big basket or bowl!

I had a very special relationship with my grandmother. As the years passed, things changed as they always do. Grandma passed away and her home was torn down. My mother salvaged the old white porcelain door knobs from this great old house, and one Christmas gave one to each of her five children. Into the hole which attached the knob to the door was placed dried rose buds and baby's breath from her garden. As a very special table decoration in each of our homes, it reminds us of times gone by and a very special and loving grandmother.

Sandra Abdallah

As a little "post Christmas letdown" surprise, sneak an ornament onto the tree of someone special with a little tag, so they know who it's from (or you can skip the tag if you want to keep it a surprise). When the decorations are being taken off their tree, the little gift is found, and so is a smile.

At Christmas time while decorating, we make "Christmas Soup". Stir into your potpourri pot some decorating leftovers, such as bits of pine, cedar berries, a cranberry or two, pieces of orange left over from orange peel ornaments and whatever else might smell nice. You can also freeze or dry these "bits and pieces" and enjoy Christmas Soup anytime until spring.

Linda Kopisch

Cut out of green felt or a green tablecloth the outline of a Christmas tree (make it large enough to fit on a door or a wall). Take Christmas cookie cutters and trace outlines on poster board or other heavy paper. Cut out the shapes. Place the shapes in a basket with crayons and a roll of tape. When little visitors come to your home, or on days when nothing will entertain your children, let them color the shapes and affix them to the tree.

Patricia Kinghorn

A Cozy Country Christmas

We place a 3' high artificial pine tree in a whiskey barrel planter. The tree is then decorated with popcorn strings, cranberry strings and pinecones dipped in peanut butter, then in birdseed. After decorating, place a bright red bow on top, and give nature a gift too...the deer and birds love this tree and we continue to stock it throughout the winter. Of course, you could use a live pine as well!

Jacqueline Lash-Idler

For a great table arrangement or centerpiece, take an old decoy and arrange evergreen boughs around it, adding an evergreen wreath with a bow around the decoy's neck.

For a fireplace, I use my old sled and arrange my collection of santas on it, placing evergreen boughs and poinsettias around them.

Sherry Hawkes

There is always a "little bit of kid" in all of us. I have surprised my co-workers with Advent calendars to count down the days until Christmas. You would be surprised at the excitement they cause in the office. Everyone gets into the holiday spirit. I usually buy them after Christmas, at half price sales, so that the expense isn't too great for the next Christmas.

Pat Akers

I have a grapevine tree that I decorate for each season. My 4-year old daughter considers it her own tree. At Christmas, she decorates it with the ornaments that have been given to her, or the ones that she has made in daycare. During the fall, we decorate with pumpkin and scarecrow ornaments. We have hearts for Valentine's Day, bunnies for Easter and red and blue homespun hearts for the 4th of July. It always has little white lights and a tin star.

Leigh Vaughn

I live in California, so to fight back those "January blues" I get after I pack Christmas away, I started a snowman collection. Not only do they make cute Christmas decorations, I keep them out right through January! It does snow in California...or does it?

Gayle Masingale

Take the branch trimmings from the tree and put into vases, pitchers, mugs and other containers. Add artificial red berries, then hang small colored glass balls. This really brings the Christmas spirit to every room in the house. It's like having a mini Christmas tree for each and every room. The "bouquet" in the kitchen has small cookie cutters tied on with red ribbon, too!

I have many different kinds of potpourri which I store in glass jars. At Christmas time I add a festive ribbon to the jar and line them up on the mantel, or on a shelf on the bookcase, where the glass sparkles and catches the light.

Diane Dollak

I have a collection of tiny angels (wooden, glass, porcelain, etc.) and an old pottery crock. Each year I fill the crock with greens and place it in the foyer, with the angels on the boughs...my angel tree! I wasn't going to put it up one year and all the kids said, "What, no angels?" They enjoyed the angel tree more than I thought they did. This tree goes up right after Thanksgiving so that we can enjoy the season a bit longer.

Therese Gribbins

I use the holidays as a time to replace all my small household plants. I remove the plants and fill small pots all over the house with boxwood, cedar, fresh holly, tansy, and mint. If you pack the greenery in, you will have a candle holder for a tall red taper candle. It is a wonderful way to have the scent of Christmas everywhere. And for special dinners and the days close to Christmas, you can have a festive candle holder. Don't leave candles unattended, greenery does become quite dry after a few weeks!

Anne McKinney
Gooseberry Patch Artisan

Gilded fruit and vegetables add sparkle and elegance to your holiday centerpieces. With gold spray paint, give a festive touch to artichokes, mini pumpkins, gourds and pomegranates. Make sure you spray paint in a well-ventilated area or outdoors.

A Cozy Country Christmas

I buy dwarf evergreen trees, on sale, at the end of shrub planting season and plant them in large clay pots. They can be placed on balconies or porches with bright bows for the holidays. They stay green all winter and can later be planted. If the pots are large enough, the trees can stay in the pots for a couple of years and make portable landscaping.

Linda Lockwood

I like to choose a Christmasy plaid ribbon and make dozens of bows for accent around the house. I use them on my tree and for wreaths, along with cedar roping inside and out. I even use the same ribbon to tie up bundles of greens, dried flowers and dried berries to hang over doorways.

Pat LaFlame

For my holiday decorations I like to use some of my favorite antiques and lots of greenery tied with bright ribbons. I place garland on the stairway, and fill a large copper bowl on my dining room table with pinecones and greens. By my front door, I place an old sled with a pair of old ice skates hanging on it and a tiny pair of old mittens. I think the natural things that we live with make the most beautiful decorations if you have a bit of imagination.

Georgene Kornreich
Gooseberry Patch Artisan

I look forward to your new books! Ever since I "found" Gooseberry Patch, I now give a copy of **Old-Fashioned Country Christmas** as part of a wedding gift or first Christmas gift to young couples. I add Christmas ornaments, holiday napkins and other fun things they might not splurge on for themselves. Many young brides love to collect things (one bride loves teddy bears, cows and apples and her sister collects mice and chickens) and to receive holiday theme goodies just thrills them.

Beverly Botten

I like to attach small jingle bells to the handles of gift bags. They add that special holiday touch. I've also put jingle bells on the dog's collar and my baby's shoes are apt to get some this year as well!

Kara Kimerline

Bring the scent of the holidays into your home. Stud thin-skinned firm oranges, lemons or limes with whole cloves. Use a nail or skewer to start holes. Add row after row of cloves until fruit is covered. Makes a wonderful decoration or centerpiece and lasts for weeks.

Graters and cookbooks, combined with candles and a little bit of evergreen, make a festive look-ing kitchen table. Set candles aglow in old graters.

Tie antique buttons on the branches of a small tree, then make small bows and hot glue them on. It's a good way to keep the buttons in the family.

Linda Tittle

I especially like to decorate the mailbox for Christmas with a fresh wreath or a spray of Christmas greenery and a big red bow I reuse each year.

Each year I choose a special decorating theme which I coordinate through-out the house. This year's theme is natural. I've strung a greenery garland on my front porch and along the railing of the back porch, tucking in herbs from my garden. I have a beautiful North Carolina Frasier Fir on which I've strung cranberry and popcorn garland and apple-cinnamon ornaments (made with cookie cutters), along with dried apple slices tied with raffia. The tree lasts longer outside in the cool air and we can enjoy it because it's just outside our kitchen window.

Mary-Gail King

Buy a small second-hand tree (recycle) and decorate your dorm room. You can use small objects from your sorority...pictures of "sisters", pins, pen-nants or a garland of sorority colors. Have family members each send you a small, nostalgic trinket that will bring a smile to your heart, and share these memories with your sorority sisters as you decorate your tree.

Wednesday Young

A Cozy Country Christmas

I have a large antique chalkboard by my front door on which I write seasonal messages like "Christmas is Coming", "Welcome All", "Christmas was Here", "Welcome Home Mark", "Give Thanks", whatever. It is so much fun and everyone loves to see what it says. I also have a small one in the kitchen for fun messages like, "Good Job", "Love You" and my Dad's saying, "B.V.K.T.E.O (Be Very Kind To Each Other).

Drape your bannister and staircase with garland. Decorate with gingerbread boys tied with homespun, orange and apple slices, yarrow, pinecones, tin cookie cutters, tiny baskets, tiny white lights and homespun bows. On the outside of the stair risers, place an assortment of individual antique tart tins. Place a votive candle in each and surround with cranberries. These are also darling used individually on a table or in the bathroom.

Fill old (or new) stockings and mittens with greens, cinnamon sticks, and berries and hang anywhere you need a country touch.

A Christmas tree without popcorn and cranberry strings just isn't a Christmas tree.

Janie Lusk

Two years ago, after Christmas, I bought a beautiful artificial Christmas tree for practically nothing. I used the branches to decorate my shelves. I also cut up artificial garlands and tucked branches in arrangements, on shelves, clocks and even the chandelier. Try putting some bare twig branches in with the artificial, adding apples, berries, whatever you choose...it takes very little time and the effect is wonderful.

When we bring home our live Christmas tree, we also bring home a load of fresh cut spruce branches (you can get these for a small price, or for free). Before we start to do our Christmas decorating, I cut the spruce branches into 1 to 2 inch pieces. I then put the cuttings into a one quart pot of cold water, bring to a boil and then let simmer for 1 or 2 hours. You may have to add more water, so keep checking the pot. Make sure to use an old pot, because it will be discolored afterwards (I use the same pot from year to year). Keep a pot simmering all through the season. Not only will your house smell wonderful, but you will be putting much needed humidity back into the air.

Sally Kennedy

Our living room Christmas tree is decorated with white lights and old ornaments collected over the years, along with fresh baked gingerbread men and animals tied on with homespun ribbons. Metal cookie cutters tied with ribbon make wonderful ornaments for the tree as well. I also like to weave long strings of raffia around the tree branches, like garlands, and tuck small bouquets of baby's breath throughout the tree. The overall effect is charming!

I frame an indoor doorway with evergreen garlands decorated with gingerbread figures, dried apples, cinnamon sticks and homespun ribbons. I also include Christmas tree lights with the garlands.

Several years ago I purchased a set of Christmas dishes. We use these all through December instead of our everyday dishes.

We collected several Christmas tapes and records over the years and play them constantly throughout December. We especially like instrumentals which might have been heard during the 18th and 19th centuries. These give a wonderful "old-time" atmosphere to the holidays.

Nancie Gensler

Tuck herb bundles in an evergreen tree and dust with angel hair or baby's breath.

Fill a small crock with unshelled nuts and add sprigs of greenery.

Load a graniteware colander with red apples and a pineapple for a Williamsburg centerpiece.

Decorate a rosemary tree with tiny ornaments, baby's breath and small spice cookies.

Fill a vase with cut eucalyptus as a natural air freshener.

Judy Carter

Holiday garlands for your mantel or table are easy to make. Using florist's wire, attach lady's apples, tangerines, lemons and limes to a pine garland, weaving french wire ribbon in and out amongst the greenery. For an old-fashioned look, string cranberries on wire and weave throughout your garland.

81

A Cozy Country Christmas

If you have allergies or do not enjoy having a fire in your fireplace, arrange a grouping of pillar candles of red, green and white on a cookie sheet and place on top of the grate in the fireplace. Accent the candles with sprigs of holly and pine to cover the cookie sheet. The glowing candles create a peaceful atmosphere. I have found this idea to be very practical, yet attention grabbing.

Susan Harvey

Purchase various size artichokes and place them on a shelf in the closet for several weeks to a month. They will shrink, but dry with a tannish brown color. Nice for dried arrangements, potpourris or strung as garlands.

Betty Monfort

I have a collection of rubber stamps in seasonal designs. I love to stamp everything, from monthly calendars, stationery, envelopes, bills, my checkbook register and small notecards. It gets me into the holiday spirit, and it even makes paying the bills a little more fun!

Nancy Rootland

Christmas packages wrapped in brown paper and tied with raffia are so simple, yet so special. Cinnamon sticks can be attached to add a wonderful aroma.

Donna Lopez

Stack several footed cake plates on top of each other to display cookies, finger sandwiches and other holiday favorites at your parties. Add washed holly leaves to each level or for a fall party, put your dip in a small hollowed out pumpkin and set on the top plate.

Sharon Andrews
Gooseberry Patch Artisan

Purchase mini candy canes in the long, clear cellophane wrappers (the kind that are usually hanging on display racks). Tie on red and green bows between the candy canes. Hang them on the wall by your front door, along with a small pair of scissors. As guests leave, cut off a candy cane for them to take with them. You can also do this with small homemade gingerbread men. Simple, just wrap them in a long strip of plastic wrap!

Lisa Glenn

When I give a handcrafted gift, I always attach the business card/logo of the crafter of the gift (usually with a tiny gold safety pin). I also leave any such tags attached to the gifts I purchase for myself, as I feel it adds to the "specialness" of the items. Throughout the year, I like to buy unique items for friends with a special collection. That way, at Christmas there are all sorts of little treats for these friends.

As I love poinsettias, I always have several for the holidays. A way to display them for a primitive look is to set them in plain brown bags, fold tops of bag down and tie with homespun ribbon or strings.

Joyce Newburn

We should all be concerned about the earth and the environment and be thinking "green". To have an environmental Christmas, buy a good artificial tree that lasts for years. If you want to use a real tree, after Christmas, remove the tinsel and put it by your bird feeder as a shelter for the birds. You can also collect the pine needles for potpourri and mulch the tree when you're through with it.

Another idea for an environmental Christmas, instead of using wrapping paper, make drawstring bags in different sizes and fabrics. They can be used year after year to "wrap" your gifts.

Margaret Clark

A Cozy Country Christmas

It's hard to know what to do for widows, widowers or divorcees at Christmas. You can always invite them to your celebration, but not force them. Just a note with a poem, song or quote will let them know that you still love them and are thinking about them.

Lisa Harmon

When sending your Christmas cards to friends and relatives you won't be seeing for the holidays, send along a small herbal tea bag with this note:

I cannot sit and chat with you
the way I'd like to do.
So brew yourself a cup of tea,
I'll think of you,
you think of me.

It will make you feel warm and cozy thinking of them.

Decorate for the holidays by using your baskets! Mount them with their bottoms against the wall, then display small collectibles or handy items such as spices, towels or dried flowers.

Eleanor Makulinski

Every Christmas I buy a loaf of fresh baked, sliced bread from the bakery (they always add a little green food coloring in the dough for the holidays). Using a small Christmas tree cookie cutter, I cut out trees on each slice. For a very pretty presentation, I serve the cut-outs toasted on a Christmas platter, with strawberry jelly in a Christmas bowl and a Christmas spoon.

Grace Meletta

Enclose Christmas confetti in your Christmas cards for a festive holiday surprise!

Dottie Dobbert

I have a very special friend who does not do any cross-stitch or quilting, so instead of sending a Christmas card to her, I quilt or cross-stitch a special ornament. I date and initial each one. She can enjoy my "cards" year after year!

Patti Rodgers-Johnson

Homemade Gifts From The Heart ♥

•Easy Holiday How-To's•

Suet Treats for Birds

Barbara Bargdill
Gooseberry Patch

1 1/4 lb. suet
1/2 c. crushed peanuts

1/2 c. sunflower seeds
1/2 c. cracked corn kernels

Melt suet in saucepan (yields about 2 cups liquid fat). Stir in peanuts, sunflower seeds and corn. Spoon into heart molds, insert straw at top (for hole); or spoon mixture into hollowed out orange halves to make a basket (attach pipe cleaners or string for the handle and hang from a branch). Cool in refrigerator until solid. If using molds, unmold, remove straw, thread with string and tie to a branch.

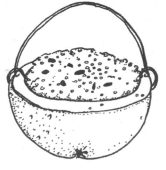

Christmas Potpourri

Joyce Newburn

My potpourri blend smells just like Christmas!

dried orange peels
dried flowers (any red petals)
dried pine, cedar, etc.
bittersweet leaves and berries
tiny pinecones (also a few
   larger ones)
rosehips berries

cinnamon sticks
anise stars
allspice
cloves
cinnamon oil
rock salt (as the fixative)

I have no definite amounts of each ingredient...simply mix until you get the desired aroma for the amount of potpourri you are making. Large batches are best and do keep well in a covered glass jar (such as restaurants get supplies in). When adding the rock salt, use approximately 1/2 c. per gallon of potpourri. Keep mixing by turning the jar every so often. Wonderful for gifts...I put mine in tiny brown sacks, tins, or whatever suits the occasion.

Growth Charts

Frannie Meshorer

It's fun to see how our children have grown and here's an idea for a growth chart. Have a special place to mark your child's height each Christmas Day, using red and green markers on alternating years. Don't forget to date! If you're a family that moves often as military families sometimes do, make a "portable" growth chart by using a 6 foot length of muslin to record their measurements.

Homemade Gifts From The Heart

Homespun Rag Garlands

Karen Ford

At Christmas time I enjoy making rag garlands. You'll need 2 yards of material (a blend of 3 different patterns works best) and 4 to 6 feet of twine. Cut or tear fabric in 2"x4" strips and tie onto the twine, any knot that you feel comfortable with will work, and remember to alternate your patterns. The length of your garland will vary according to how tightly you "pack" your pieces. These homespun rag garlands will look great on your Christmas tree, fireplace mantel, window and as curtain tie-backs! Choose your fabrics to suit any season.

Candy Wreath

Sheryl Pearson

Take a 5" embroidery hoop, either plain or painted red. Next apply a generous layer of tacky glue at the seam of the inner and outer hoop. Press approximately 17 to 18 pieces of peppermint candy close to each other, covering the entire surface of the hoop. As a final touch, apply a decorative red ribbon to the top, with long tails. I've even added a bell to the center to make it more Christmasy. It's very inexpensive to make and you have a darling Christmas decoration.

Yuletide Potpourri

2 c. pine needles	1 c. bay leaves
3 T. rosemary	1 T. whole cloves
dried orange peel	cinnamon sticks
tiny pinecones	berries
2 T. ground orris root	14 drops cinnamon oil

Mix dry ingredients in a ceramic or glass bowl. In a separate container, stir together the ground orris root and cinnamon oil. Add this to the dried mixture. Toss gently. Allow to cure for 2 weeks in a tightly closed container in a cool, dark place. Shake occasionally.

•Easy Holiday How-To's•

Old-Fashioned Salt Dough Ornaments

Marie Alana Gardner

These salt dough cut-outs look great in an old yelloware bowl or basket.
Here's the recipe: **2 cups of flour**
                1 cup of salt
                1 cup of water

Mix until dough forms. Cut out gingerbread men and add raisin or whole clove buttons. Bake at 350 degrees for about 25-35 minutes, until dough is hardened. Cool and spray with clear enamel. Tie bows around their necks, using scraps of calico or homespun.

Popcorn "Ornament" Balls

Evelyn Kovalovsky

Use 2" (or any size you prefer) styrofoam balls. Using an electric hot air popper, pop up some plain (not buttered) popcorn. Hot glue the popcorn to the styrofoam ball, covering the entire ball. Let dry. Take gold string and form a loop on the popcorn ball so that it can be hung on the tree. It gives the effect of snowballs hanging from your tree. For a more festive look, use colored popcorn kernels. Making popcorn ball ornaments is a great craft activity for children.

Homemade Christmas Potpourri

Sally Kennedy

For Christmas, I like to make my own Christmas potpourri. Use whatever you can get in the grocery store (spices, apples to slice) and in the fields (pods, pinecones). Then get a very good scented oil (cinnamon, orange, anything you like) and blend in a glass jar. After a couple of weeks, add orange peel, cut into star shapes using a small 1" star cookie cutter (use a hammer to tap the cutter through the fresh, clean rind). Fill cellophane bags with the potpourri, tie with a ribbon, and place in a huge wooden bowl. Everyone loves these little take-home gifts.

Holiday Centerpiece

Deena Funk

For a quick (no sew, no glue!) centerpiece for Thanksgiving last year, I sat a grapevine wreath on the table, "scrunched" autumn wrapping paper inside it, tucking under the edges, and filled the lined wreath with wooden apples, pinecones and a little raffia. It looked so good, I kept it out all year! For Christmas, I used the same wreath, only added berries and a small Father Christmas doll tucked in between the apples and cones. The look can be varied by simply changing the wrapping paper lining.

Luminaries

Jacqueline Lash Idler

On Christmas Eve, we (and our neighbors) line our walkways and driveways with paper bag luminaries. It's such a beautiful, bright, warm and friendly way to welcome the Christ Child's birth. You'll need:

> **sand**
> **votive candles**
> **paper bags (lunch bags)**

Simply pour 1 cup sand into bag. Place a candle in the sand and light. The luminaries should burn 1 to 2 hours.

Jewelry Tree

Mickey Johnson

Cut out a green felt Christmas tree and decorate with old clip-on earrings (with clips removed) or old jewelry. The jewelry I used was worn by my mother and grandmother and brings back good memories of loved ones who are no longer with us. I framed the tree and hang it up every Christmas.

•Easy Holiday How-To's•

Instant Memories
Deena Funk

As family and friends come over during the holidays, take an instant snap-shot of them around the tree, table, or outside in the snow. Have some pretty metallic or designed paper on hand and mount the snapshot onto the paper. Trim edges of mounting paper with pinking shears. Have your guests deco-rate the edges with sequins, stickers, dried berries or flowers, etc. Then use colorful markers to write in the date and occasion at the bottom of the picture (in the white rectangular space). Your guests now have a personalized, dated ornament to take home with them. Especially fun for the kids.

The Art of Sharing
Rebecca Suiter

I look at garage sales, flea markets, and antique shops for pretty, inexpen-sive containers to place homemade cookies, cakes or candies in. I then give them as gifts to my friends, along with this message:

Do Not Return To Sender
Friendship is the art of caring.
Friendship is the art of sharing.
When this plate is empty and the goodies are all gone,
Fill it again for another friend, so you can pass it on.

I decorate the message with one of Gooseberry Patch's Christmas rubber stamps.

Love Ties
Linda K. Zell

My mother gave me some ties that belonged to my dad (he had passed away suddenly) for my husband and son. Since they already had quite a few ties and these ties were too beautiful to dispose of, I decided to make them into a unique and sentimental gift. I found an artisan who opened up each tie, pressed it, then cut it into pieces. After she had pieced and stitched them together, she then made pillow forms, and found some very nice fab-ric (almost a houndstooth, very masculine) for the backing. Each pillow ended up being about 10"x15". For the first Christmas without my father, I gave my mother and sister each one of the pillows. There was surprise, tears and much reminiscing. This truly was one of the best Christmas gifts I have ever given, and I am sure they will become family keepsakes.

Recipe Greeting Cards

Yvonne Bendler

I've always included a recipe with my Christmas cards. A few years ago I decided to do a mini-cookbook Christmas card. Here's how you can make your own:

- Take a sheet of typing paper and fold it into quarters. When cut, this will make an 8 page cookbook. If a 16 page cookbook is desired, use two sheets of paper.
- Type up your recipes and have your local copy shop reduce them to fit the size of the pages. (If you've used an 8 1/2 x 11 sheet of paper, your cookbook pages will be 4 1/4 x 5 1/2 after folding.)
- Next, cut out the printed recipes and glue them onto the pages with a glue stick. So that your recipes will be going in the right direction, make up a dummy copy of your book before you start. Get as creative as you like by decorating around your recipes with borders, if you choose. Another fun idea is to use your rubber stamps to stamp on lots of country charm after your book is assembled. Decorate the front panel as the greeting page.
- Now it's time to photocopy your pages. Make as many copies as you will need, and remember to copy on both sides of each sheet so that your recipes will be back to back and going in the right direction in your book.
- Cut your pages in half and carefully machine sew up the center of the card to hold your pages in place. You can then flip through the pages to see all your wonderful recipes!

This is a fun and really inexpensive way to share some favorite recipes with loved ones. The only problem is that once you start sending recipe greeting cards, your family and friends won't let you stop. Mine tell me they look forward to my "Christmas Calories" every year and it's a card that is never thrown away.

A Gift of Good Taste

Jere Piper

A few years ago for Christmas, I decorated recipe boxes with "Mom's Favorite Recipes," "Aunt Jere's Favorite Recipes," and "Mrs. P's Favorite Recipes" (depending who I was sending them to) and gave them to our children, our nieces and nephews and the young married children of our friends. Each year I send them recipes from a different food category along with a corresponding gift, like a cookie plate for cookies, casserole dish for casseroles, salad bowl for salads, etc. The young people say they look forward to seeing which recipes will be next and I love doing it!

•Easy Holiday How-To's•

Yummy Bean Soup

Rori Hillman Jensen

A pint canning jar filled with ingredients for a hearty 10 bean soup makes a thoughtful, healthy and economical gift for a hostess, drop-in friend or a neighbor. Fill a pint (2 cups) canning jar with the beans. Cut some pretty Christmas material in a circle and place over the seal before screwing on the band. Include the recipe by writing it on a 3"x5" card and slipping it into an 8 oz. size disposable baby bottle liner. Now the recipe is in its own protective plastic, safe from spills. Trim off the excess plastic then use a hole punch to punch through card and bag. Finally, tie the recipe to the jar using ribbon. Your friends will think of you as they eat this delicious soup on a cold winter's evening.

Great fillers for gift baskets are sachets, potpourris, candles, ornaments, cookie cutters, tiny boxed candies, teas, cinnamon sticks, spices, sugar shakers, wooden spoons, kitchen gadgets, homespun towels, seeds, fragrant soaps, bubble bath, gourmet jams, jellies, etc.

Light fades
Stars appear
Evening angels
gather here

Spiced Rag Balls

Pam Riemer

styrofoam balls
*several 1/2 inch strips of
    cotton fabric
ground cinnamon

ground allspice or cloves
ground nutmeg
glue gun
melon ball utensil

Cut each styrofoam ball in half and hollow out the centers, using the melon ball utensil. Leave approximately 1/4 inch of the outer shell intact. Place approximately 1 teaspoon of cinnamon, 1 teaspoon of nutmeg and 2 teaspoons of allspice or cloves in the center of one half of the ball. Place the 2 halves together and use the glue gun to secure them if desired. Wrap each ball with fabric strips, covering the ball with one layer only. Secure the end of the fabric with glue.

*If you use balls smaller than 2 inches in diameter you will have to decrease the width of your rag strips. For very large balls you may want to increase the rag strip width.

Quick Gingerbread House

Carolyn Ritz Lemon

For a quick gingerbread house, use icing to attach the graham crackers to each other. Decorate with candies, marshmallows, etc. Recycle a foam tray (from your supermarket) and use it as a base for your gingerbread house. With some help, the children will enjoy making their own "handcrafted" gift, made with love. Here's an easy icing recipe for "gluing" your gingerbread house walls together:

3 egg whites, room temperature
1/2 t. cream of tartar
16 oz. pkg. powdered sugar, sifted

Beat egg whites and cream of tartar until foamy. Add sugar gradually, mixing well. Beat for 5 to 7 minutes. Keep covered with plastic wrap at all times as this icing tends to dry very quickly.

•Easy Holiday How-To's•

Christmas Fragrance

Barb McFaden

I make this potpourri yearly and I double the batch so I have enough for myself for the year and also enough for gift giving. It is wonderful because it is so natural.

1 c. orris root chips (purchase at health food or craft store)
1 1/2 c. crushed cinnamon sticks
1 c. whole allspice
2 c. dried orange peel
1 c. crushed bay leaves
1 c. coriander
1 c. mint-spearmint

1/2 to 1 c. cloves
1 c. star anise
1 c. pine needles
1/2 c. rosemary leaves
30 drops cinnamon oil
30 drops clove oil
1 small bottle orange oil

Put the orris root in a glass mayonnaise jar. Add all the oils, shake and let sit, with lid on, for one week. In a large industrial size pickle jar, add all the rest of the ingredients and shake. At the end of the week, add the orris root to the rest of the ingredients. Let it age for awhile. Add up to 1/3 cup of potpourri to a simmering potpourri burner and enjoy! It will cost you only $25-$30 for a year's supply.

Christmas Lightbulb Necklace

Lisa Glenn

16 round beads (clear, white, red and green)
cording or ribbon (about 30")
3 colored Christmas lightbulbs (red, green and blue)
a drill

Drill a hole in the metal base of each bulb (the hole needs to be drilled cross-wise). String onto the cording beads, lightbulb, beads, etc., until all are used. Make a knot in the cording on each side of the beads to hold in place. Knot the ends of cording together to finish the necklace.

Kids' Creations

Denise Turner

Preserve "special" artwork from your preschooler with contact paper and hot glue a magnet on back for smaller projects. For larger masterpieces...buy your own mat and frame and give grandparents an "original". Your child will be very proud to give something he made and you know how excited grandparents will be!

Homemade Gifts From The Heart

Candy Tree

Lisa Glenn

We always had a candy tree at my house when I was growing up!

styrofoam cone
straight pins

individually wrapped candies
ribbon

Using the straight pins, attach the candy to the styrofoam cone starting at the base. Overlap the upper rows of candy onto the lower rows, enough to cover the pins. Put a bow on top of the tree with a pin as well.

Potpourri Ornament Balls

Michelle Hogan

water soluble glue
2 c. potpourri

styrofoam balls (any size)
skewer

Grind potpourri into small pieces (you can use a food processor). Insert skewer in ball. Cover ball with glue and roll it in potpourri. Pat to make sure it sticks onto the ball. Some of the glue will show through, but it will dry clear. You can add a ribbon and hang it on the tree or put a bunch of them in a basket or bowl. The fragrance lasts all year round.

Scented Holiday Baskets

Pam Riemer

Take several white birch logs (2 or 3 inches in diameter). Cut each log into 1/2 inch diagonal slices with a table saw (approximately at a 35 degree angle). Place scented oils on each slice and place the wood pieces in your holiday baskets with pinecones, greenery and berries. For an added sparkle, dust your birch pieces with diamond dust glitter.

•Easy Holiday How-To's•

Handprint Apron
Sheri Berger

Make a special gift for the teacher. Have all the kids in the class put their handprint on a white cotton apron in bright colors of paint. Use a permanent marker or fabric paint marker to have them sign their names next to their handprint. Iron over the finished apron once to permanently set the paint. This is also a wonderful idea for grandma.

Orange Peel Ornaments
Michelle Golz

Create orange peel ornaments by peeling the orange in as large sections as you can. Cut in strips (1/4" wide) and wrap tightly around a pencil. Leave on the pencil until dry (about 4 days or so). Glue on ribbon with glue gun or poke hole for string before drying. Gives a corkscrew effect and smells delicious!

Cinnamon Stick Bundles
Linda Tittle

A perfect touch for a package decoration or for a tree trimming ornament gift. Glue together 3 cinnamon sticks in a bundle and tie with a festive ribbon. Your friends and family will love this homemade touch.

Potpourri Christmas Bulbs
C. Denise Green

I purchase clear glass Christmas bulb ornaments and fill them with my homemade potpourri. Then I make a small bundle of everlastings and hot glue them to the top of the bulb. Tie on a pretty bow and ribbon hanger and you have a wonderful gift for family and friends.

Candy Cane Vases
Dottie Dobbert

Attach candy canes (approximately 24-5 1/2") to empty soup cans (label removed) with a hot glue gun. Do not remove cellophane wrappers, they will help prevent damage and protect candy from water. Tie a ribbon around the middle. Use as a vase for holly...or fill with soil and plant a paperwhite narcissus bulb (4-6 weeks before Christmas). Makes a nice hostess gift.

Santa's Enchanted Reindeer Food

Judy Gidley

Every year, my son and I make about 500 Christmas cards, giving one to everyone we know. He does the calligraphy and I hand stencil each card. I attach each card to a bag of "Santa's Enchanted Reindeer Food" that I make out of pinestraw and grass clippings. I put these in a paper bag and spray them with "snow" (and hairspray for stickiness). I then sprinkle glitter and foil confetti on the pinestraw and clippings. I staple it with our labels containing a cute poem about feeding reindeer and the directions:

1. Wait for Christmas Eve.
2. Just before bedtime, place the Reindeer Food out with Santa's cookies or open and sprinkle on your lawn.
3. Hop into bed.
4. Shh. Listen for Santa.

CONTENTS:
Enough magical hay for 9 tiny reindeer.
Not for human consumption.

I punch a hole in the back of each card and attach it to the bag with jute. On the 23rd and 24th of December, I ride all over town delivering my reindeer food and Christmas cards. It is so much fun to give a present to grown people and little children that brings a smile to their faces. Some of my friends have parent/children parties. I deliver the food and card at that time to them. This year I will wear my tennis shoes that I've made into reindeer shoes, my reindeer antlers and my reindeer sweat shirt and hand out the "food" to my kids.

Reindeer Feeding Poem:

'Tis the night before Christmas,
Santa will soon be here.
We give cookies to Santa,
Now let's feed his reindeer.

•Easy Holiday How-To's•

Festive Candleholders
Linda Desmond

4" styrofoam ball (cut in half)
1- 12" candle (match color to fabric)
1/2 yd. fabric (cut into 2" squares; color may vary depending
   on holiday)
glue
pencil

Push candle into center of cut styrofoam ball (ball should be flat side
down). Place color side of fabric square on the pencil point, hold it in place,
dip in some glue and push into ball. Cover the entire ball with the fabric.
Makes a beautiful candleholder. I have made these in Cub Scouts and in my
classroom as presents for mom! Even the youngest child can make these
and beam with pride. Use the same procedure with styrofoam wreaths,
balls, trees and even on straw wreaths.

The Twelve Days of Christmas...Stories
Sallee Walker

A gift idea given to me by a friend was a collection of twelve short
Christmas stories copied on red and green paper and rolled into scrolls, with
a note attached that read:

We give you a special gift for your family to share;
Hope it brightens up your season and spreads joy through the air.
For the twelve days of Christmas as you gather around the tree;
Read a story to your family, and I'm sure you'll agree.
It will be a fun tradition, every night til Christmas Day;
It will fill your hearts with love that will never fade away.

Some of the stories I had heard before, others were new to me. My children
love to choose one and hear a heartwarming story about Christmas and the
season. Many women's magazines carry great stories, or even the newspa-
per may have an interesting Christmas article. Find twelve stories of your
own and give this gift of time to those you love.

> *Cranberries, an old holiday culinary and tree-trimming tradition,*
> *can be used to decorate wreaths and topiaries too!*
> *Simply string them on floral wire and the strands can be used in*
> *arrangements and bent to fit any design.*

98

Christmas in a Jar

Kristen Eddy

Decorate around the lid and just under the screw tops of a blue or green antique canning jar, with a selection of dried Christmas greens, holly, canella berries, small pinecones, rosehips, herbs and beautiful ribbon or homespun bows. Fill the jar halfway with fresh cranberries. Carefully insert a votive candle (cranberry or cinnamon spice) in the midst of the berries and continue adding cranberries to the rim of the candle. A wonderful gift for the host and hostess of all your Christmas gatherings.

Fragrant Holiday Ornaments

B.J. Myers
Gooseberry Patch

I like to bake these and wire them into garlands and wreaths for a fragrant holiday.

1 1/4 c. flour
3/4 c. mix of cinnamon
    & cloves, ground
1 c. salt
1 c. water

The 3/4 cup of spices can be changed to a spice or spices of your preference. I tend to use about 1/2 clove and 1/2 cinnamon. Mix all together, then knead. If too sticky, add more spice, not flour. Roll dough out on well powdered surface (again, I use cinnamon, not flour). Roll to 1/2" thickness and cut with cookie cutter. Place on a baking sheet covered with parchment paper or lightly sprinkled with cinnamon. Bake at 350 degrees for about 25 minutes (plus or minus depending on the thickness). You will have to check for hardness. When cool, you may paint with acrylic paints and coat with a spray acrylic finish (if you do this it will cut down on the fragrance). Don't forget to poke holes with a straw before baking.

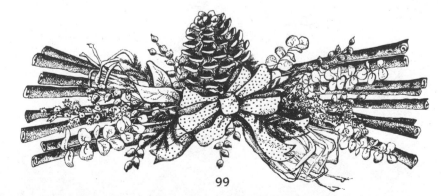

•Easy Holiday How-To's•

Gingerbread Cookie Bowl

Amy Natale

Use your favorite gingerbread cookie recipe. When dough is rolled out, shape it over a small stainless steel mixing bowl, shaping as needed to create a bowl shape. Cut small shapes out around rim of dough (which is still on the bowl). Put bowl (inverted) and dough, into a preheated 325 degree oven. Cook for 20-25 minutes. Remove from oven and let cool. Remove bowl CAREFULLY and you now have a gingerbread bowl to serve the cookies you make with the remaining dough.

Gingerbread Decorations

Rosalie Sporrer

Use a brown paper bag and cut 2 large gingerbread shaped people. Place a single layer of quilt batting between them and stitch all together with brown thread 1/8" from edge. Decorate with raisin eyes and nose as well as raisin buttons down the front, and stencil on a red heart. Use spray glue on the front and quickly sprinkle with cinnamon. Use white frost fabric paint about 1" in from edge of feet and hands to do a squiggle design. Finish off with a raffia tie around the neck. I've hung mine on the wall, but a basket of several of these is also darling. They are also lovely attached to a gift package. A super country accent!

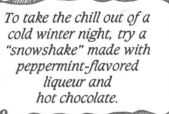

...LET IT SNOW...

To take the chill out of a cold winter night, try a "snowshake" made with peppermint-flavored liqueur and hot chocolate.

☆'Tis the Season☆

Last November on the day after Thanksgiving, I welcomed the holiday season in with a unique celebration. Instead of my usual weekly "girls-night-out," I opted for a "girls-night-in" and hosted a Potpourri Party. I invited a small group of close friends (most of whom are stressed-out moms) to my home asking each person to bring two ingredients...one purchased and one found around the house or yard. They were also asked to bring a special treat in the form of food or drink to share with the group. We had a fire, drank champagne, nibbled on shrimp, laughed, told (uninterrupted) stories and had a great time while we mixed up two huge bowls of Christmas and Kitchen potpourris. Everyone left the party with healthy samples of each potpourri to use themselves or to give as gifts. I think they also left feeling merrier and a little pampered before the joyful, but stressful, season began.

Store-bought items to choose:
cinnamon sticks
cinnamon oil
bay leaves
rosemary
ground orris root
whole allspice
whole nutmeg
star anise
lemon balm
balsam or fir oil

Things found around the house:
orange, lemon and lime peels
homegrown herbs & spices
dried apple & orange slices
large pinecone chunks
tiny pinecones
pine needles
holly berries
cranberries
bayberry
juniper
cedar
boxwood

Being one of ten children can be a bit stressful at Christmas time. Between our own children, our friends, my husband's family and my rather large family, shopping can turn into a nightmare. To relieve some of this burden, my brothers and sisters started a new tradition a few years ago that is more fun and practical than buying each other gifts. We choose names out of a hat and are strongly encouraged (yet not required) to make each other's gifts. Some of the more creative ideas have included video tapes (homemade, of course!), audio tapes, homemade foods, scrapbooks, Christmas decorations, woodworking projects, decorated baskets, wreaths, homemade jewelry, silk and dried floral arrangements and even poems have been exchanged. Last year my brother went so far as to dig up some old drawings my college-age niece had done when she was of preschool age and wrapped them up for her to open. This added a funny and thoughtful moment to everyone's Christmas night.

Joanne Martin-Robinson
Gooseberry Patch

The following event occurs every couple of years, several weeks before Christmas. I live in an old log house in the woods, which dates back to the early 1800's. My mother and I invite our friends for an ornament-making party. Work tables are set up in the den, living room and dining room and each table is stocked with the necessary supplies and equipment to make a specific ornament. After much chatter and laughter, lunch is served. Creating usually continues through and after lunch. The result...guests go home with three handmade ornaments, they find themselves deep in Christmas spirit, and they've made a new friend or two while fighting over the glue gun!

Deborah Mooney

My sisters and I like to host our family "Progressive Dinner". Christmas Eve and Christmas day are very often hectic, busy times, and each of us has our own spouse's families to visit. We decided to set aside a day prior to Christmas, to travel from house to house, visiting. This way the children get to see all the trees decorated and it's a great way to enjoy pre-Christmas festivities, while gearing up for the big day. We each have a suitable dinner course...appetizers at the smallest house so we can mingle, main course at the house with the longest dining table, and desserts at the house where wonderful desserts are made! It works out very nicely and gives us a special day to celebrate the season together.

Cathy Marcquenski

Every Christmas, a group of us ladies gather at someone's home for a "Christmas Craft Exchange". The craft has to be homemade and we set a price. We serve Christmas cookies and punch and draw numbers to see who gets what craft. I never would have believed how talented we are. Each year we try to out-do ourselves and always add a few more ladies to the group.

Margaret Riley

☆'Tis the Season☆

When my brother and I were young, our mom made surprise balls, filled with candy and tiny toys. I have continued this tradition with my own children, as the first present to be opened on Christmas morning. I use red crepe paper for my one son and green for my other son. Since they are teenagers, I place baseball card packages, pens, foil wrapped chocolates, ornaments and sports related gifts between the layers of crepe paper. The boys have as much fun finding each little gift as I have in making the surprise balls, and preserving this joyful tradition.

Priscilla Golz

My husband and I come from large families and Christmas is spent with many relatives. We decided to make New Year's Eve our special holiday with our seven children. New Year's Eve day is spent preparing snacks and decorating for the festivities. Throughout the evening we play games and enjoy our snacks. At 10 o'clock, we prepare black-eyed peas that are eaten at midnight for good luck in the coming year. When the clock strikes twelve, we have a toast to our family and then each child gives a toast of their own. We wind up the evening by shooting off fireworks!

Teresa Breitensteir

Each year my father would read Dicken's, **A Christmas Carol** to us in the evenings before going to bed. This would take a full week and the story would end on Christmas Eve.

Mickey Johnson

Be sensitive to the needs of our senior citizens this holiday season. It's not the crystal bud vase or the silk pajamas that they want... it's you. Spend some time together, perhaps a trip to the mall to hear the Christmas music, a ride in the car to enjoy the Christmas lights, services at church, lunch at a favorite restaurant or give coupons for snow shoveling, grocery shopping or getting them to the doctor. If you live far away and can't be together, a much appreciated gift would be a basket filled with a box of all-occasion cards, a pad of lined paper, stamps, pens and plain envelopes or how about a "big print" book or a magazine subscription. Also, don't forget gift certificates for groceries, long distance telephone calls, electric or gas service for a month or a visit to the beauty shop. Remember, a visit and the words, "I love you" can mean more than you would ever imagine!

We have a tradition in our family that started many years ago by my mother called "Santa's Sleigh". We have a santa doll and a little wicker sleigh, which sit on a table filled with tiny, but brightly colored, decorated packages. There is one package in the sleigh for each friend and family member who will be sharing Christmas dinner with us. The gifts are not opened until Christmas evening when we are having dessert. Then one of the children gets to pass out a gift to each person. It could be a pair of earrings, a small bottle of cologne or a toy. The gifts are small, but everyone looks forward to opening them, especially the children, because even after all of the festivities of Christmas day, they know that they will still have one gift left to open.

Linda Day

The spirit of Christmas is very dear to me, and I always feel that the spirit should last for longer than the month of December. I love to bake bread, so on the first day of every month in the year, I give "baked goods" as gifts to my friends and relatives. I often co-ordinate the treat with a special holiday for the month. This way my special holiday spirit lasts throughout the year.

Patti Rodgers-Johnson

Our family has enjoyed a tradition started by my grandparents long ago. All year long, grandma collected wind-up toys of all kinds. On Christmas day, after our presents were opened and the dinner dishes cleared from the table, we each sat down for our "Jack Horner Pie". Grandma attached each toy to a string, with a gift tag on the other end. The toys were put in her clothes basket, strings hanging over the edge, and the toys covered with tissue paper. Simultaneously, we pulled the string with our name on it. Merriment and much laughter came when we wound up our toys. To this day my family enjoys our Christmas "Jack Horner Pie", only now the grandma is me!

Nancy Campbell

Four years ago I had an idea which has become a Christmas tradition at our house. Throughout the year I purchase small, inexpensive items such as keychains, costume jewelry, little toys or cassette tapes. Before Christmas, I wrap and tag the boxes and arrange them on a decorated tray. After Christmas dinner, while family and guests linger over dessert and coffee, I sneak upstairs to get the tray of "dessert gifts". It's a nice surprise at the end of the day and helps make the Christmas magic last a little longer.

Anne Farnese

Remember when you were a little kid and right after a snowfall, what fun you had? Couldn't you still just lick your lips for a snow cone made with freshly fallen snow? Or, how about making snow angels or building a snowman. Remember how good it felt to come inside, fingers and toes stinging from the cold, to take off those frosty clothes, sit by the fire and sip a cup of hot cocoa? Find that little kid inside you and relive some of your happiest childhood memories!

106

In our town, we have a "Tree of Life". Some places call it a "Giving Tree". Written on each paper ornament is a description of a needy person and what he or she needs or would like for Christmas. We each choose an ornament with someone about our own age and buy that person a gift, usually something they want, because it makes it a little more special for them. Sometimes, my two boys give an additional item, something they themselves would like to have. Giving a gift to someone, not knowing who is receiving it, gives us a special feeling.

Elenna Firme
Gooseberry Patch Artisan

One December afternoon after school, our staff members got together in the art room and made "Joy" sweatshirts. Each person brought fabric scraps, laces, trims and paint to share. Even though the same letter stencils were used for the word "Joy", each shirt was different and unique. We wore our shirts on the last day of school before Christmas holidays. The children loved seeing "Joy" everywhere they looked. After school, we all gathered together for a group picture. It was a wonderful way to share in a joyous season and it was the best faculty picture ever!

Judy Roque

It is an old Victorian tradition, which originated in Germany, to hang a glass pickle ornament on the Christmas tree. It was always the last ornament to be hung on the tree, with the parents hiding it in the green boughs among the other ornaments. When the children were allowed to view the tree on Christmas morning, they would begin searching for the pickle ornament. Whoever found that special ornament first would receive an extra little gift left by St. Nicholas. My daughter is almost 2 years old and this is the first tradition that she is beginning to understand. Because of that reason, I have decided to keep this and other Victorian traditions alive. This year (and hopefully many more) we are having Christmas Eve dinner at our house and young and old alike will be searching for the "pickle"!

Dawn Ross

☆'Tis the Season☆

This is a tradition my husband started 10 years ago when we got married. He would go to the local greenhouse and buy me a beautiful poinsettia plant. It got to be a little more special when our daughter was born, because now the two of them would go together to buy it. But the best part is when there is a knock at the door and there stands my daughter holding the poinsettia saying, "This is for you Mommy!", with a big smile on her face and my husband standing behind her with tears in his eyes. I hug them both and my little one always asks, "Why are you crying Mommy?", and I tell her, "Because I love you and Daddy very much!" I hope this tradition will always continue.

Jackie Bankovic

Taking down the Christmas tree is always such a sad experience. I used to hate watching our three boys' sad little faces stare at the barren tree, as it lay on the ground outdoors waiting to be hauled away. Then I had an inspiration! Why not let the boys adorn the tree outdoors for the animals. On the designated day, I give each boy a small jar of peanut butter with a plastic knife, a squeeze bottle of honey, and whatever kind of cereal or crackers we have in the house. We take the tree out and the boys have a ball painting the tree with peanut butter and drizzling it with honey! Then they throw handfuls of cereal or cracker crumbs on the tree, and of course, it sticks to the honey and peanut butter. Once finished, we get hours of enjoyment watching from the windows as an assortment of birds and squirrels come to enjoy our Christmas tree.

Kim Estes

My church has continued a very meaningful tradition. After the children's Christmas service, all of the young participants are given their "Christmas Bags". Each bag contains an orange, apple, popcorn ball, small bag of candy and bag of peanuts. The bags are just plain brown paper and tied with white string. Our church began this tradition in the Depression, as possibly, the only Christmas gift many of the children would receive. The tradition has continued to this day, to remind the children of how precious these gifts, simple as they may seem, were to the children of such difficult times. Thinking back, I still vividly remember the lovely smell as those bags were opened, and I give thanks for the plenty that has filled my blessed life.

Laura Steuk-Mastropaolo

When my parents initially divorced, we children were quite young and, as most children are, penniless. So my father began the annual tradition of taking us all holiday shopping for our mother. He would graciously fund our expedition and then take us out for a terrific dinner. We have continued this tradition but, unfortunately, we now purchase our own gifts. He has continued to spring for the festive dinner out though!

Jacqueline Lash-Idler

To help eliminate our children always asking to open a gift early, we started our own "Twelve Days of Christmas." In each Christmas stocking goes twelve stocking stuffers. We start on December 13th and each morning, before everyone goes their separate ways, we get to open one stocking stuffer. The last one is opened on Christmas Eve. Christmas day is then left to open all the gifts under the tree.

Ann Davis

A favorite tradition that we have passed onto our daughter and her family involves cutting down the Christmas tree each year. We pack either a breakfast or a picnic lunch to have in the woods after we get our tree. How nice it is to have a winter picnic, complete with fire to cook bacon or hot-dogs. Yum-Yum!

Carrol Begley

☆'Tis the Season☆

Growing up during the 40's and 50's I remember the excitement of preparing for Christmas. As Christmas Day neared, my uncle would stop by evenings to tell me that he had been talking to Santa's elves, who were watching from the roof to make sure I was being good. About two weeks before Christmas, my mother and I would walk to Pemberton Market, or the used car lot, to pick out a Christmas tree. We would then carry it home because we had no car. Then the tree would be decorated with old glass ornaments...a few of which I still use. My mother would hang artificial poinsettias in the windows. The fresh turkey, wrapped in white paper, was bought at the local meat market. My mother's stuffing was a simple common cracker stuffing with onions and Bell's seasoning. On Christmas Eve the turkey would cook all night in the oven of our black iron stove, on the heat from the burners that heated the house. Mashed potatoes, squash, peas and cranberry sauce would be served...a simple, but elegant dinner. An annual event would be to take the train into Boston to look at window decorations in Jordan Marsh and Filene's and then on to Boston Common to see the lights and Nativity scene. Some of these traditions are still carried on at my home. To quote from the song sung by Dean Martin, "memories are truly made of this."

Dorothy Hender

Every year, since my two girls were born, I buy or make two photo Christmas ornaments. I then put a current picture of them in the ornament and date the back. We have fun putting the ornaments in chronological order to see how they've changed and grown.

Linda Youngren

Bake a Christmas pudding, an old English tradition! For luck, add a tiny horseshoe charm; for wealth, a silver coin; for marriage, a silver ring. Whoever gets the charm in his or her dessert has good luck in the coming new year!

110

☆Favorite Memories & Traditions☆

My husband and I have very close friends that, like us, love to go to garage sales and flea markets. We decided to start a new tradition with these friends. Every Wednesday the gals get together to go to the sales, and all during the garage sale season we buy little treasures, secretly, for the other two couples. We set a dollar amount to be spent on each. We then take turns, in December, hosting a simple dinner and then the fun begins. We exchange all of our flea market and garage sale finds, which have been wrapped in anything they will fit in. We have a wonderful time opening all the silly and sometimes great surprises.

Connie Carmack

The holidays are so busy and the grandchildren seem to receive so many gifts from Santa. So my husband and I suggested we start a tradition of having the grandchildren open their gifts from us on Christmas Eve. After church, the children come home, settle down with hot chocolate and cookies, and open their special gifts from Gram and Gramps. This way it makes the holidays seem a little longer and more special. It gives them a chance to realize what Gram and Gramps gave them instead of the gifts being lost in the excitement of Santa's larger gifts. People on fixed incomes can't afford large gifts, especially when they have several grandchildren, so this special time makes their gifts seem more important and much more fun. When some of the grandchildren live far away, this also makes a special time on Christmas Eve to remember the grandparents who sent the gifts.

Several years ago on Christmas Eve, my daughter said in fun, "You all should drop by my house in the morning because Bob (my son-in-law) is making breakfast burritos for us." So after they left, we all planned an early morning "surprise visit" for my daughter's family. We all went home, looked into our refrigerators, and took any breakfast food we could find. It turned out to be a family tradition to have "Christmas Breakfast Burritos". We gather at different homes on Christmas morning and eat breakfast together. This also gives everyone a chance to join the other sides of their families for an afternoon or evening visit. A lot of families are not the "early morning riser" types as our families are, so this gives equal time for everyone.

Pat Akers

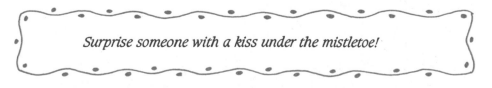

Surprise someone with a kiss under the mistletoe!

☆'Tis the Season☆

Each December, purchase a warm winter coat from a thrift store. Put the coat over your arm and go to a park or area where homeless people gather. Sit on a bench for a few minutes and thank God for your blessings. Then leave the park...and the coat. A homeless person will find it and be grateful. You might want to tuck inside one of the pockets, an envelope with "meal money" and a note wishing the finder blessings. In warmer weather, pack two lunches, go to the park and eat your lunch. When you leave, place the second lunch on the bench in a bag, for someone less fortunate than you. Hunger knows no season.

Wednesday Young

After Thanksgiving, it's been a tradition for my nine grandchildren to come to grandmother's farm home to decorate their own gingerbread houses. I love the holidays and for the children it's a special time. I delight in this quality time with them and as the years go by, the teenagers enjoy this decorating session as much as the little ones. The look on their little faces as they decorate will always be remembered in my heart. And I know that making the gingerbread houses will provide wonderful memories for my grandchildren, who call me "Ava", Portugese for grandmother.

Theresa Brazil

My daughter's birthday is in December, which gives us a great reason to have a gingerbread house party. I pre-bake the houses and assemble them ahead of time, so that when the children arrive, the table is covered with assorted candies to use as decoration. Each child has a bowl of icing with a butterknife and their own house to decorate as they please. No matter how young or old, the houses all turn out beautiful. The houses also become the Christmas centerpieces for their homes for the holidays!

Kathy Lafleur

☆Favorite Memories & Traditions☆

My mother loves almost anything Victorian, and has a collection of demitasse teacups. Believing that we all need to learn to relax and enjoy traditions of another time, she started serving Christmas tea for her grandchildren. They are invited to participate as soon as they are old enough to go to the cupboard and choose their favorite cup for teatime. Each child may pour their tea and choose from a selection of tiny sandwiches, petit fours and cookies. Candles are lit and classical music is played. No matter the age, the grandchildren catch the mood of this special time, and look forward to this special quiet time for conversation and old-fashioned fellowship during the busy, hectic holidays.

Sheryl Valentine

One of our family traditions at Christmas is for Santa to leave a jigsaw puzzle (1000 piece) under the tree. This becomes the family "project" for the next few days and helps extend the Christmas holiday, bringing young and old together to help complete the puzzle. It's also been the reason for some late nights for the adults!

Kathleen Popp

A special Christmas tradition started by my father about 35 years ago was to paint a Christmas scene on one or more of the windows of our house. He would use washable paint and choose a picture from one of our favorite Christmas cards. One of my sisters and I carry on this tradition, and even get our kids involved. They help pick out the picture and even help paint. By drawing a picture on banner paper the size of your window, you can tape the paper to the outside of the window, while you're painting. It is even possible for the kids to help with the painting this way. Though Dad is not here to share the tradition, we feel he is with us in spirit, when we relive this special Christmas tradition.

Pat LaFlame

Tangerines and the fresh fragrance of pine bring back childhood memories of Christmas. What scent brings Christmas back for you?

113

☆'Tis the Season☆

We put up our Christmas tree early in December. I leave the boxes of ornaments out and whenever one of the children does a "good deed", he can choose an ornament to hang on the tree. With five good children, it's not long before the tree is decorated!

On the eve of December 5, we all leave our shoes out for St. Nick. He puts a sweet (usually dates rolled in coconut, but sometimes other treats) in each shoe and leaves a little note too. Sometimes someone (Dad or Mom) gets a shoe full of potatoes, onions, garlic or coal, and the children have a good laugh on us!

Diane Dollak

We intentionally extend our tree decorating project to last for a week. The first night we all pick out the tree at the nursery. The second night we bring the tree into the house and enjoy the evergreen smell. The third night the lights are put on the tree. The fourth and fifth nights the ornaments are put on the tree by the entire family. Each ornament is taken from its separate sack with its identifying information (where purchased, year, gift from ___, etc.). With each ornament we reminisce about the people, places and Christmases past, sharing that history with our son. These evenings are always accompanied by Christmas music.

Linda Arndt

One night during Christmas season why not say, "No TV tonight," turn out the lights, tell Christmas stories and "remember when's" and talk by the lights of the Christmas tree.

114

☆Favorite Memories & Traditions☆

Since we live in a very rural area and don't see our neighbors very often, we make Christmas baskets for each of the surrounding families each year, and deliver them as a family. They are usually a small bag of pumpkin and holiday breads made in coffee cans and flower pots, teas and coffee mixes, a package of hot chocolate, and a few handmade ornaments. It's always a fun touch to add a few stems of fresh daisies and greenery and a big holiday bow. It is a great way to stop and give a warm holiday wish, and let people know that you care.

Anne McKinney
Gooseberry Patch Artisan

We have no children, but certainly enjoy the children of our friends. Instead of trying to keep up with their desires and interests, in order to provide them with a Christmas gift that will be enjoyed and not outgrown, we've chosen to deliver gifts that will stand the test of time. We give them unusual, handmade ornaments that we have discovered in our travels. Sent out the day after Thanksgiving with instructions to be opened when they put up the Christmas tree, these gifts have created a couple of unexpected surprises. First, their parents are forced to be efficient about decorating for the holidays, because the children plead to open the gifts. And, after 20 years of this, my friends realized that when the children move away from home, they are going to have a naked tree!

Judith "JJ" Jamison

Each Thanksgiving my children receive early Christmas gifts. Our two sons and daughter, and their families, spend the holiday evening at our home. I collect Christmas decorations and clothing (after Christmas sales or I make them myself during the year) and give these to them at Thanksgiving. This way, they enjoy their gifts all of December and a year doesn't go by before they can use them.

Neta Liebsche

115

☆'Tis the Season☆

Ever since the boys were small, I made up a game of "Can you find the
_____ ornament?" Considering that my Christmas tree has over 500 ornaments, it took a lot of patience. The boys love every minute of it. Now the
neighborhood children all come over to play. But as my boys got older, they
would find the ornaments too fast. I had to move the ornaments around
when they weren't looking. To my surprise, one little girl started playing it
at her house! They never get too old to play. My sons are now 15 and 10
and still we play, one last time, the night before we take the tree down.

Linda Desmond

After my brother and I both got married and had families, and the
Christmas lists grew longer, we decided to have only the kids exchange
gifts. Instead of buying gifts for the adults, we use the money to meet in the
city (San Franciso) and have an afternoon of shopping and a nice dinner.
Each year we try a new restaurant. We truly enjoy it and look forward to an
evening out (and the kids look forward to a night at Grandma's with the
cousins). For us, there is nothing like the week before Christmas in the city,
with a cable car ride and Union Square store windows.

Gayle Masingale

When I was a little girl, our biggest thrill at Christmas was tree hunting. All
the family, sometimes our northern cousins as well, would all go down to
the old family farm and pick out the best cedar tree around. Years later, as
an adult, I still enjoy this tradition with my extended family. This is an all
day outing, because, how could you possibly take the first tree you see! We
then all troop back to our home for hot buttered rum, hot chocolate and big
bowls of chili.

Rebecca Chrisman

While growing up, my sister and I always put up a small Christmas tree in
our shared bedroom. We put our presents to each other under this tree and
they were always the first ones we opened on Christmas morning. This tradition continued even after my sister moved away from home to attend col-
lege, but would visit for Christmas vacation. It was a special time just
between the two of us.

Suzanne Carbaugh

Traveling through Lancaster, Pennsylvania this fall (Amish country), we noticed that many homes had small electric candles glowing in each window. It looked so cheery and welcoming...almost like someone waving hello from inside the house. Now we have also adopted this tradition for harvest and Christmas seasons in our home in California. These candles are relatively inexpensive and not hard to find. Here in southern California we need to keep a candle burning to show a little warmth to our neighbor or to that stranger passing by.

Andrea Redeker

One of our family traditions starts a week before Christmas. Our children participate in doing "extra" jobs around the house and in return are paid for doing these tasks. After they have earned enough money, they buy a toy and donate it to "Toys For Tots". We think this helps our children to learn that giving to others is what Christmas is all about!

Tina Main

We make sure that as a family we watch our favorite Christmas movies. We make plenty of popcorn and wrap ourselves in blankets, and enjoy!

Phyllis Schantz

☆'Tis the Season☆

If you would like to keep in touch with family more often than just at Christmas, start a family letter. Make a list of participating family members and their addresses. The first person on the list writes a letter and sends it to the next person on the list. After reading the letter, they add their own and send the two letters on to the next family member on the list. The last person on the list sends all the letters back to the first person on the list. They take out their old letter and insert a new one. One week is a good time to limit for each family to write down their news and get the family letter back in the mail. We keep our old letters in a binder for our own family journal. We also send pictures and good recipes with our family letter.

Lisa Glenn

This buffet has been a tradition with our family for years. We had six children, so Christmas was a very busy time for us. It didn't take me long to realize that a sit down meal with these kids was a big mistake. They were so excited and wanted to be playing with their toys. So, I would set up this buffet and when they were hungry, they could help themselves. Most of this can be made the day before. This gives moms time to enjoy their family. The buffet includes potato salad, baked beans, gelatin fruit salad, meatballs, sliced ham, rolls and bread, and an assortment of Christmas cookies for dessert.

Georgene Kornreich
Gooseberry Patch Artisan

We have saved all the Christmas books that my daughters have had since they were little. Each year we put them out in various places around the house for all to enjoy. Each year I also add one or two new books. Children and adults alike enjoy looking at these books and, often, they bring back pleasant memories of times past.

Sherry Obenauf

Each Christmas season we have a large (1000 piece) jigsaw puzzle going on a table. Each visitor in and out during the holiday is asked to put a least one piece in and sign their name on a piece of paper. When the puzzle is finished, it's glued to a board, with the signature paper and year glued to the back to keep track of the contributors!

Sheri Berger

Besides buying gifts for friends and family, try to remember those less fortunate. Every year, my husband and I donate food to the community kitchen and pet food to the local animal shelter. Giving of yourself is much more spiritually rewarding than receiving presents.

Margie Clark

Our family has been keeping a "Holiday Memory" photo book of all the Christmas parties and dinners for over 25 years. The children and grandchildren love to page through all the memories of good times shared...a wonderful legacy to pass on.

Kristin Ammermann

Recipe for Love

1 1/2 cups happiness	1 quart kindness
2 cups thoughtfulness	1 Tablespoon thankfulness
2 Tablespoons consideration	1/4 teaspoon attention
1 gallon help	6 pinches obedience

Mix all; blend until smooth. Bake in your heart. Will serve 365 days for a lifetime.

Linda Tittle

Cheer up that person living alone in a nursing home by making them a "Joy Box". Each year I fill a box with 25 inexpensive wrapped gifts, such as candies, books, homemade preserves or canned vegetables, socks, cards, Christmas candles or ornaments, holiday dish, sample-sized lotions or soaps. The ideas are endless and the kids love to help. Give this box of goodies to someone special on December 1st and they will have something to look forward to every day until Christmas. This time of year can be very lonely for some, so spread that good cheer!

C. Denise Green

Don't forget to decorate your bedchamber with pine, wreath, trees, white twinkle lights, candles, Christmas books and a cozy red plaid blanket for the holidays.

☆'Tis the Season☆

Our gift exchange is very special to us! For the past 10 years we have had a "Treasure Hunt" with one gift for each child, with 5 or 6 clues. Before they were able to read, we drew pictures for the clues. This "hunt" is very convenient for large, hard-to-wrap gifts. One year, I wrapped each person's gifts in a certain type of paper, but did not put names on any packages. When we opened the gifts, I gave each person a swatch of their paper and then they knew which gift was theirs. Another year I named each member of the family a reindeer. The gifts were tagged "To: Rudolph, To: Dancer", etc. On Christmas Eve, I told them what name I had given them. This year the children thought I had finally "acted normal" and just tagged the gifts as they should be. However, on Christmas Eve, after they had had a week to try to figure out what was in their packages and were about to open them, I told them that the labels were reversed. All of Brittany's gifts were really for Nathan and all of Nathan's gifts were for Brittany. Christmas is such fun!

Suzanne Dodd

My mom and dad, all the children with our families, and even some friends, rent a cabin that will fit us all, near a special attraction (ours is a ski slope). Menus are planned and we all share in the grocery shopping and preparation of a great sit down dinner, together as a big family again. Of course, when we kids go skiing, we have instant babysitters, who usually go sledding with the grandchildren. And at night (this is my favorite part) we play puzzles or games and sit around talking, like a family again. This is so therapeutic and many of us don't ever want to leave.

If you are lonely at Christmas, volunteer to work in your school system. Children will make you feel young and they need your help too. Just volunteer at your favorite school and let them know what you like to do...tutoring, office help, lunch line, fundraisers, playground supervisor, library, etc.

We have a blessing jar in our home. When an event happens that is special, we write it down on a piece of paper and put it in this jar. Then at a time when we feel all has forsaken us, we open up that jar again to remember how much we are blessed.

Lisa Harmon

120

☆Favorite Memories & Traditions☆

We have an inexpensive dime store manger scene up on our mantel. Every year we add a figure, so you can imagine after 40 years how special and how crowded it has become. There is the set of oxen that our son carved when he was in Cub Scouts, a pinecone angel, clay doves that sit on the roof, a set of brass camels from Turkey, two little carved pine trees, a wood cutter carved in Canada, and on and on. It's great fun and looks delightful. There's even a little santa.

Carol Kinghorn

When the day's Christmas cards arrive, I place them on the dining room table. That evening during grace, we ask the Lord to bless (by name) the individuals that sent the cards, during the coming year. The cards are then placed in a decorated basket in the living room, for family and friends to read and enjoy.

When my parents moved to Florida from the north, my sister and I decided to surprise them with Christmas stockings. The first year, along with their Christmas package, we sent simple felt Christmas stockings with their names in ironed-on letters. We included favorite soaps, different small items and regional favorites that would be difficult to find in their area. An example would be apple cider mix, a small can of "real" maple syrup and mill-ground flour. Each year they look forward to their Christmas stocking surprises.

Anita Van Horn

If there is a church in your community that offers midnight candlelight service, try to attend. When I was a child, my mother, grandmother, aunt and I would make an event of it. It truly made an impression with me about the true meaning of Christmas. When everyone in the congregation had their candles lit, we would sing "Silent Night". Whenever I hear that hymn, I get a warm feeling in my heart.

Terrolee DeMenge

My family has been spending Christmas Eve together since long before I was born (I am now 36). There are 46 of us who join in the traditional meatless meal, which usually includes a variety of fishes. After grace, my grandfather (now deceased) would always say, "Whoever eats the fastest eats the mostest!" My uncle has taken over saying the traditional phrase, but I'm sure all of us still hear Grandpa's voice.

Donna Lopez

☆'Tis the Season☆

In our large family we exchange filled Christmas stockings. We fill a stocking for each member in the family. The women/girls fill one with items for a woman or girl and the men/boys do the same. We place our names on the stockings, bring them to our holiday gathering, and place them under the tree upon arriving. We put each person's name in a bowl, one bowl for the females, one for the males, and each member chooses a name. We delegate the passing out of the stockings to a family member, who acts as santa's helper. When the name on the stocking is called and you drew that name, that is the stocking you receive. It is quite a sight to see 15-20 filled stockings under the tree and see the excitement generated, from the oldest family member to the youngest. You can be as serious or as silly as you like with the items you choose to fill your stocking. And for the next year, you know you'll be filling the stocking again, and can pick up items throughout the year. This has worked really well in our family and we have a lot of fun doing this. We also include our friends who may be with us on our day. All they have to do is bring a filled stocking and share in the fun along with us. I am going to suggest doing it at the office this year.

Marsha Downs

My three granddaughters, aged 9, 6 and 2, come every year to decorate our tree. As they grow, the decorations climb higher on the tree. I always leave the tree just as the girls decorated it, because the memories are better than a perfect tree.

Jackie Samo

As the four siblings in my family (including me) grew, my mother began a wonderful and fun tradition. We are always looking for fun "family" things to do together, and she creatively combined family togetherness with stocking stuffing. Instead of filling stockings herself, she gave everyone an envelope with equal amounts of cash inside, with instructions that we were to purchase a small stocking gift for each member of the family. We were to find gifts that matched his or her personality, of course. We headed to the local mall, had a time limit of 2 hours, were told to make the money "stretch" and find appropriate gifts. As we are all married and live far apart, this has become a favorite activity when we head home for Christmas. It's almost as much fun dodging each other in the stores, as it is finding the right gifts. When home, we have a wrapping party...wrapping, labeling and stuffing everyone's stocking (often with hilarious gifts). We can hardly wait for Christmas morning to see what everyone gets.

Deena Funk

⋆Festive Food & Drink⋆

Veggie Bars

Deborah Donovan

Delicious and nutritious!

1 can crescent rolls
8 oz. cream cheese
1 c. mayonnaise
2 T. ranch dressing

6 c. raw vegetables (cauliflower, broccoli, carrots, green pepper, etc.)
parmesan cheese

Press crescent roll dough into 2 13"x9" pans. Bake at 350 degrees for 10 minutes. Cool crust. Mix cream cheese, mayonnaise and ranch dressing together and place on top of crust. Chop vegetables and place on top of dressing mixture, and sprinkle with parmesan cheese. Cut into squares.

Mushroom Turnovers

Judy Borecky

Crust:

8 oz. cream cheese
1 c. margarine
2 c. flour

1 egg white
sesame seeds

Blend together and chill.

Filling:

1 lb. fresh mushrooms washed and
    chopped fine
1 c. chopped green onions
2 T. margarine
1/4 t. thyme
1/2 c. sour cream
1/4 t. salt
2 T. flour

Saute mushrooms and onions in margarine for about 4 minutes. Add the rest of the ingredients, cooking for a few more minutes. Roll out dough and cut with a biscuit cutter or a round cookie cutter. Place less than 1/2 teaspoon of mixture in the center of each circle. Fold over and seal edges by mashing all around with a fork. Brush each turnover with beaten egg white (one will be enough), and sprinkle over sesame seeds. Bake in a preheated 350 degree oven for 12-15 minutes. These freeze well. Makes 50 - 60 turnovers.

Barbecue Meatballs

Suzanne Carbaugh

This recipe was given to me by my mother, Nancy Campbell, and is a great hors d'oeuvre or potluck dish. There are never any left over!

1 lb. ground beef
1 slightly beaten egg
1/3 c. fine, dry bread crumbs
1/2 t. poultry seasoning

1/2 c. catsup
2 T. brown sugar
2 T. vinegar
2 T. soy sauce

Mix ground beef, bread crumbs, egg and poultry seasoning. Shape into about 2 dozen 1 1/2" balls. Brown balls slowly in a greased skillet at medium-high heat. Pour off excess fat. In a small bowl, combine catsup, brown sugar, vinegar and soy sauce. Pour over meatballs. Simmer; stirring occasionally, for 30 minutes. To serve, insert one toothpick (I use frilly ones) into each meatball and place on a serving plate.

Party Rye Appetizer

Eleanor Makulinski

8 oz. pkg. cream cheese
1/2 pkg. dry salad dressing mix
(garlic, onion, or Italian)

1 party rye bread
1 cucumber

Combine cheese and dressing mix. Spread on slices of party rye, then top with cucumber slices. Refrigerate until ready to party.

Pizza Fondue

Michelle Golz

Serve warm in fondue or chafing dish (or even simmering in a crockpot on low) with toasted french bread slices!

1 onion, chopped
1/2 lb. ground beef
2- 10 oz. cans pizza sauce or
    1 jar of spaghetti sauce
1 T. cornstarch
1 1/2 t. fennel seed

1 1/2 t. oregano
1/4 t. garlic powder
10 oz. grated cheddar cheese
8 oz. grated mozzarella cheese
2- 1 lb. loaves french bread,
    cut and toasted

Brown onion and hamburger in a large skillet. Drain fat; add remaining ingredients and simmer. Yield: about 2 quarts or enough for 2 pounds of bread.

✦Festive Food & Drink✦

Tangy Barbecued Meatballs

Linda Zell

2 lbs. ground round
1 c. cornflake crumbs
1/3 c. parsley flakes
2 eggs
2 T. soy sauce

1/4 t. pepper
1/2 t. garlic powder
1/3 c. catsup
2 T. instant minced onion

Sauce:

16 oz. can jellied cranberry sauce
12 oz. bottle chili sauce, regular

2 T. brown sugar
1 T. lemon juice

Mix ingredients and form into small meatballs. Put in 13"x 9" pan. Set aside. In sauce pan over medium heat, mix sauce ingredients, stirring until smooth and cranberries are melted. Pour sauce over meatballs and bake uncovered for 45 minutes at 350 degrees.

Tennessee Caviar

Beverlee Wallace

3 cans black eye peas
1 can white hominy
1 1/2 c. chopped onions
1 c. chopped green onions,
    stems and all
2 c. chopped green pepper

2 medium tomatoes
1 T. garlic
1 T. parsley
1 small can green chilies
2 c. Italian dressing

None of the ingredients need to be drained. Combine all ingredients; marinate for 24 hours. Salt and pepper to taste. Use as a dip with crackers or tortilla chips.

Mushroom Rolls

Ann Fehr

1 3 oz. package cream cheese
1 3 oz. chopped mushrooms
1 pkg. crescent rolls

Roll out rolls (don't separate), spread mixture onto dough, separate, roll up and cut into thirds. I freeze on a cookie sheet. Once frozen, place in a freezer bag and use as needed. Bake at 350 degrees approximately 20 minutes.

Tortilla Roll Ups

Suzy Roberts

These keep well in the refrigerator and are actually better the next day. Great to keep on hand for parties and unexpected guests.

1 pkg. flour tortillas
1 block of cream cheese, softened
1 bunch green onions

Cut off the ends of the green onions, wash and pat dry. Chop the onions into small pieces. Cream together the chopped green onions and the cream cheese. Spread onto flour tortillas and roll up (jelly roll fashion). Let these tortillas sit covered in your refrigerator for about 1 hour, or until firm; slice into bite-size pieces. Dip into salsa.

Salsa

Sheryl Desrocheis

1 large can whole tomatoes,
    drained and chopped
1 medium onion, chopped
3 jalapeno peppers, chopped
1 oz. white vinegar

1 oz. lime juice
1 T. garlic salt
1 T. oil
1 T. cilantro

Combine above ingredients. Chill and serve with your favorite taco chips. Wrap in plastic wrap and tie with a festive ribbon.

✦Festive Food & Drink✦

Stefan's Cheese Ball
Diane Dollak

A cheese ball with crackers is great to take to a party or to give as a holiday gift!

12 oz. cream cheese
6 oz. blue cheese
1 can pitted black olives, drained and well chopped
2 T. sherry, if desired
1 can mixed salted nuts, chopped

Mix everything but the nuts well and form into 2 or 3 balls. Roll in the chopped nuts until they are absorbed into the cheese and cover the balls.

Bacon Treats
Marsha Downs

1 lb. bacon
1 can water chestnuts
1/2 c. mayonnaise-type
   salad dressing
1 c. brown sugar
1/2 c. chili sauce

Cut bacon and water chestnuts in half. Wrap water chestnut with a slice of bacon, secure with a toothpick. Place in a 13"x9" baking dish. Mix all other ingredients together, pour over water chestnuts. Bake at 350 degrees for 45 minutes.

Cheese Strips
Terri Burdoff

1/2 lb. sharp cheddar cheese, grated
6 slices bacon, cooked and crumbled
1 small pkg. slivered almonds
   (optional)
2 t. worcestershire sauce
1 small onion, minced
1 c. mayonnaise
1/4 t. dry mustard
8 slices of bread

Mix cheese, bacon, almonds, worcestershire sauce, onion, mayonnaise, and mustard together. Spread onto bread slices; cut into small strips (strips can be frozen at this point). To cook: Place in 400 degree oven for 10 minutes. Yield: approximately 32 strips.

Hot Crab Dip
Susan Harvey

1/2 lb. crab meat
8 oz. cream cheese
1/2 c. sour cream
2 T. mayonnaise
1 T. lemon juice
2 T. grated cheddar cheese
 (need 8 oz. pack)

1 1/4 t. worcestershire sauce
1/2 t. dry mustard
pinch of garlic salt
about 1/2 c. milk

Mix cream cheese, sour cream, mayonnaise, lemon juice, worcestershire sauce, garlic, and mustard until smooth. Add enough milk until creamy for dipping. Stir in 2 tablespoons cheese and add crab meat. Pour into a greased 1 1/2-quart casserole dish; top with remaining cheese. Bake at 375 degrees for 20 minutes. Serves 10-12.

Baked Baby Gouda
Leona Keeley

14 oz. baby gouda
18 oz. tube crescent rolls

Preheat oven to 375 degrees. Remove wax and thin yellow layer from baby gouda. Remove crescent rolls from tube and unroll. When unrolled, the dough forms a rectangular shape, do not separate into triangles. Place baby gouda in center of rectangle. Bring long edges of rectangle together; pinch to seal. Pinch together remaining edges of dough to completely enclose cheese. Place on a cookie sheet, bake at 375 degrees for 11-13 minutes, or until golden brown. Serve immediately.
Yield 20-22 servings.

*Potluck Christmas Eve...
everyone prepares their
favorite dish and not one
person has to do
all the work!*

✦Festive Food & Drink✦

Curried Crab Dip

Karen Freeman Bragg

3 large pkgs. cream cheese,
   softened
1/2 t. seasoned salt
1 t. onion juice
1/2 t. curry powder
1 t. worcestershire sauce
2 t. mustard (wet)

2 cans crabmeat
1/2 c. mayonnaise
1/2 t. garlic salt
1/4 c. white wine
2 t. powdered sugar

Place all ingredients in a casserole dish and stir together. Bake at 350 degrees for 1/2 hour, or until bubbly. Serve hot and cover with slivered almonds.

Grandma Muschweck's Cheeseball

Sally McArthur
Gooseberry Patch

Tastes even better when it's made a day ahead!

1 pkg. dried beef, diced
6 oz. cream cheese

dried onions, minced
walnuts, finely chopped

Mix cream cheese and dried beef. Then add dried onions to taste. Make into ball and roll in walnuts.

Spiced Cream Cheese Spread
Jacqueline Lash-Idler

16 oz. cream cheese,
   softened
4 T. butter, softened
4 T. honey
1/2 t. cinnamon
1/2 t. nutmeg
1/2 t. orange peel
1/4 t. ground cloves
1/4 c. raisins

Puree raisins with butter and cream cheese. Add honey and spices. Place in crock or desired dish. Refrigerate until firm. Great with breads and muffins.

Super Loaf
Jacqueline Lash-Idler

1 can refrigerated pizza dough
Dijon mustard
10 oz. box of frozen spinach or broccoli
approximately 1/2 lb. Monterey Jack, sharp cheddar, or Swiss
    cheese, shredded
4 slices of boiled ham (optional)

Roll pizza dough out onto greased cookie sheet; bake for 10 minutes at 350 degrees, until slightly browned. Spread desired amount of mustard onto dough; then add a layer of chosen vegetable, cheese and/or meat, leaving 1" on one end free. Roll up towards the free end, placing seam down on sheet. Cover top with foil. Bake at 350 degrees until cheese melts (approximately 20-30 minutes). Uncover for the last 10 minutes, to brown top. Let cool slightly. Slice into 1" slices. You can freeze, wrapped in foil; and re-heat in the same foil at 350 degrees for 30-45 minutes.

Polish Mistakes
Jan Kouzes

1 lb. hamburger
1 lb. bulk sausage
1 lb. pasteurized processed
    cheese spread

1 T. worcestershire sauce
1 T. oregano
1 t. garlic powder
3-4 loaves party rye

Brown the meats separately and drain well. Mix meats and add cheese and other ingredients, melting over low heat (or in microwave). Cover for cheese to melt. Spread on rye bread. Quick freeze and store in freezer in freezer bags. Bake at 325 degrees for about 8 minutes if frozen, or 4-5 minutes if thawed.

Crab Cheese Muffins
Ann Fehr

1/4 lb. butter
1 jar processed cheese spread
1/4 t. garlic salt

dash of worcestershire sauce
1 6 oz. can crabmeat
5-6 English muffins, split

Slowly melt butter. Add processed cheese spread until blended, garlic salt and worcestershire sauce. Add crabmeat. Spread on English muffins and cut into wedges. I freeze on a cookie sheet. Once frozen, place in freezer bag and use as needed. Bake 350 degrees approximately 15 minutes.

✦Festive Food & Drink✦

Open Face Cucumber Sandwiches
Ann Fehr

1 8 oz. pkg. cream cheese
1 pkg. dry salad dressing

party rye bread

Combine ingredients, spread on party rye bread and top with cucumber slices. Sprinkle with dry salad seasoning.

Raspberry Punch
Kathi Stein

46 oz. can pineapple juice
6 oz. can frozen pink lemonade
16 oz. raspberry sorbet or sherbet
2 liters ginger ale, chilled
10 oz. pkg. frozen red raspberries,
    thawed

1/2 oz. rum (optional)
1/2 oz. brandy (optional)

In a large punch bowl, mix together juices, sorbet or sherbet and ginger ale. Stir in undrained thawed raspberries. Yield: 4 1/2 quarts or 36-4 oz. servings. A decorative ice mold could be added to float in this punch. I have also substituted strawberry sorbet and strawberries for the raspberries.

Christmas Punch
Gail Hageman

1 qt. frozen strawberries, thawed
1/2 to 1 c. sugar, to taste
2 bottles white Rhine or Moselle wine, chilled
1 bottle dry champagne, chilled

Place fruit in punch bowl with sugar. Crush fruit and allow sugar to dissolve. Add wine and chill for 4 hours. Just before serving, add champagne. Makes 24 punch cups.

> *When hosting a holiday party, encourage guests to mingle throughout your home. Set up snacks and bowls of punch, eggnog and coffee in the living room, dining room, kitchen, family room and study. Your friends will be able to enjoy your holiday decorations so much more!*

Holiday Gathering

Hot Buttered Rum
Ginny Valley

1/2 lb. butter, softened
1/2 lb. brown sugar
1 qt. softened vanilla ice cream

nutmeg and cinnamon to taste
rum

Cream together butter and brown sugar. Slowly add ice cream. Season with nutmeg and cinnamon to taste. Pour into a freezer container and freeze. To serve, put a medium scoop into a large mug. Pour in a shot glass full of rum. Fill with boiling water. Sprinkle cinnamon on top and add a cinnamon stick.

Spiced Cider
Pat Akers

The aroma is fantastic!

2 qts. apple cider
1/4 c. brown sugar
1/2 t. whole allspice
1 t. whole cloves

1 cinnamon stick
1/4 t. salt
dash nutmeg
1 orange, cut in wedges

Prepare cider using a large automatic coffee maker. Substitute the cider for water. Place remaining ingredients in coffee basket with filter and brew. Makes two quarts.

Hot Spiced Tea
Juanita Williams

This makes a great drink for those cold wintry nights around the holidays. Serve to guests for tree-trimming or caroling parties.

2 qts. strong tea
6 oz. can frozen orange juice
3- 3" whole cinnamon sticks
1 t. whole cloves
1 t. whole allspice

1/3 c. honey
1/2 c. dark brown sugar
orange slices stuck with whole
   cloves for garnish

In a large saucepan combine all ingredients, except orange slices; bring to a boil. Simmer for 5 minutes. Strain and pour into warmed heatproof punch bowl. Garnish with orange slices. Makes 12- 2/3 cup servings.

Festive Food & Drink

Cranberry Mist
Juanita Williams

1/2 c. vanilla or eggnog
   ice cream
1/2 t. cinnamon

2 heaping t. fresh
   cranberry sauce

Mix in blender. Pour into cocktail glass. Sprinkle with nutmeg. Float whole fresh cranberry on top. Stir with cinnamon stick. To make fresh cranberry sauce for drink:

2 c. fresh cranberries

1/2 c. sugar

Cook until soft.

Banana Crush Punch
Linda Tittle

3 c. sugar
6 c. water
1 large can pineapple juice
12 oz. can frozen orange juice

5 ripe bananas
   (mashed in blender)
2-3 qts. ginger ale or lemon-
   lime carbonated drink

Mix together all but ginger ale. Freeze. Take punch out of freezer 1 to 1 1/2 hours before serving. Add 2 or 3 quarts ginger ale or lemon-lime drink (best with hand mixer) just before serving. Makes about 1 1/2 gallons.

Hot Cranberry Punch
C. Denise Green

3 qts. water
3 c. sugar
1/2 c. red hots
1 qt. cranberry juice

1 c. orange juice
1 c. pineapple juice
1/2 c. lemon juice
whole cloves

Heat together the water, sugar and red hots in a large pan, until sugar and red hots are fully dissolved. Add remaining ingredients. Sprinkle with whole cloves. Heat and serve. Wonderful!

Sprinkle shiny gold stars everywhere...on your tablecloth, on the packages under your tree and inside cards and letters, like Christmas pixie dust!

⋅Festive Food & Drink⋅

Applesauce Muffins

Barb McFaden

Great for breakfast, brunch, snacks or with dinner. A real crowd pleaser!

1 c. margarine
1 c. white sugar
1 c. brown sugar
2 eggs
3 t. cinnamon
2 t. baking soda

4 c. flour
2 c. applesauce
1 t. allspice
1/2 t. salt
1 c. chopped nuts

Cream margarine. Blend in sugars and eggs. Add nuts, cinnamon, soda, all-spice and salt. Mix well. Add flour and applesauce. Bake at 400 degrees for 15-18 minutes. Makes 36 or more muffins. Can be microwaved on high for 2-3 minutes (remember to rotate pan). Batter can be kept in the refrigerator for 2 weeks. Just stir it up and bake.

Grandmom Nellie's Christmas Eve Fried Dough

Phyllis Ann Schantz

My family makes this "sweet treat" every Christmas Eve. Yummy for Christmas morning too!

3 loaves frozen bread dough
sugar and cinnamon

On the morning of Christmas Eve, take bread dough out of freezer and place in a large bowl. Brush the outside with oil. Cover completely with a damp towel. Remove the towel several times and "punch" the dough down. In the evening after dinner, when you're ready for a treat, ready a frying pan with oil or you may use a deep fryer. Let the oil get very hot. While heating the oil, mix together the cinnamon and sugar, to taste, in a bowl; set aside. Roll the dough apart and drop into oil by teaspoonful; turning once. When browned, remove from oil and roll in the cinnamon and sugar mixture.

Quick Coffee Cake

Judy Borecky

1 pkg. white or yellow cake mix
4 eggs
1 small pkg. coconut or vanilla
    instant pudding mix
3/4 c. water
3/4 c. oil

1 T. vanilla extract
3 T. sugar, mixed with
    1 1/2 t. cinnamon
1 c. chopped walnuts

Using mixer, mix ingredients (except sugar, cinnamon and walnuts) until well blended. Pour batter into a sprayed 10 1/2"x13" pan. Sprinkle with cinnamon and sugar; then sprinkle walnuts and bake in a preheated 350 degree oven for 30 minutes. Drizzle icing over coffee cake and serve.

Icing:

2 T. milk
1 t. vanilla

1/2 c. powdered sugar

Whisk ingredients together well.

Easy Caramel Orange Ring

Mickey Johnson

1 T. butter
2 small jars of orange marmalade
1/2 c. chopped walnuts
2- 10 oz. cans buttermilk
    refrigerated biscuits

1/2 t. cinnamon
1/2 c. melted butter
    (set aside)
1 c. packed brown sugar

Preheat oven to 350 degrees. Grease a bundt pan with 1 tablespoon butter. Place by teaspoonsful the orange marmalade in bottom of bundt pan until covered. Sprinkle nuts on top of marmalade. In a small bowl, combine brown sugar and cinnamon; mix well and set aside. Separate biscuits. Dip biscuits in melted butter, then sugar mixture. Stand biscuits on edge in bundt pan, spacing evenly. Sprinkle with remaining sugar mixture and drizzle with remaining butter. Bake for 45-50 minutes, or until brown. Cool upright in pan for 5 minutes. Invert onto serving plate. Serves 8 to 10.

Decorate under your tree with old toys...a train, teddy or doll.
What wonderful memories this will bring back!

Festive Food & Drink

No Knead Pecan Rolls

Sheri Berger

1 pkg. dry yeast
1/4 c. warm water
1 c. milk, scalded
1/4 c. shortening
1/2 c. butter
2 T. light corn syrup
1/4 c. sugar

1 t. salt
3 1/4 to 3 1/2 c. flour
1 beaten egg
1 c. brown sugar
2 T. butter, melted
1/2 c. sugar plus 2 t. cinnamon
pecans (as many as desired)

Dissolve yeast in water. In separate bowl, combine hot milk, shortening, 1/4 cup sugar and salt; cool to lukewarm. Add 1 cup flour and beat very well with beaters. Beat in yeast and egg. Add remaining flour. Don't knead! Let rise 1 1/2 to 2 hours. Divide dough in half and roll out. Cover with 2 tablespoons melted butter and sprinkle with sugar and cinnamon mixture. Roll up tightly and cut into 1" pieces. Heat slowly 1/2 cup butter, corn syrup, and brown sugar. Sprinkle pecans in bottom of 2 cake pans. Pour mixture over the nuts and place rolls on top. Let rise for 45 minutes. Bake at 375 degrees for 20-25 minutes. Invert onto plate.

Wonderful Sausage Bread

Vicki Hudson

1 pkg. frozen bread dough
    (2 loaves)
1 lb. bulk sausage
    (mild or spiced)
2 eggs, beaten

8 oz. shredded Swiss cheese
4 T. parmesan cheese
1/2 t. garlic powder

Thaw bread dough. Cook sausage, chop and drain well. Spread each loaf of bread dough on its own greased 10"x15" baking pan (I use a cookie sheet). Mix sausage, beaten eggs, Swiss cheese, parmesan cheese and garlic. Spread 1/2 of the mixture on bread dough; press into dough. Put the other half on the second loaf of dough. Fold bread dough over in thirds lengthwise. Fold ends up and seal (this is to keep the juices inside). Place dough on a greased cookie sheet. Bake at 375 degrees for 20-30 minutes until golden brown. Freezes well. Makes two wonderful loaves.

Give a winter garden for the holidays...long after the holidays are gone, they'll still be thinking of you with wonderful fresh herbs.

Skiers French Toast

Georgene Kornreich
Gooseberry Patch Artisan

For Christmas Brunch serve with chilled juice, fresh fruit, Canadian bacon or sausage and lots of wonderfully strong brewed coffee!

1 stick butter
1 c. brown sugar
2 T. dark corn syrup
1 loaf of French bread,
   cut into thick slices

5 eggs
1 1/2 c. milk
2 t. vanilla
pinch of nutmeg

Cook butter, brown sugar, and corn syrup until sugar is dissolved; pour into a 13"x9" pan. Layer cut up bread on top of syrup mixture in pan. In a bowl mix eggs, milk, vanilla and nutmeg; pour over bread slices. Cover and refrigerate overnight. Bake, uncovered, at 350 degrees for 45 minutes.

Breakfast Pie

Sue Welch

8 slices bacon, cooked crisp
   and crumbled
1/2 c. cornflake crumbs
1 T. bacon drippings
5 eggs
2 1/2 c. frozen hash browns
1 1/2 c. shredded Monterey
   Jack cheese
1/2 c. cottage cheese
1/3 c. milk
1 green onion, thinly sliced

Combine corn flake crumbs and bacon drippings; set aside. Beat eggs until foamy. Stir in remainder of ingredients. Pour into greased 9" pie pan. Sprinkle with crumb mixture and bacon. Cover; refrigerate overnight. Bake at 325 degrees for 50 minutes. Makes 6 servings. Recipe can be doubled and baked in a 13"x9" pan.

·Festive Food & Drink·

Apple Fritters
Michelle Bellizzi

Delicious as snacks or with syrup and butter!

1 c. flour
1 1/2 t. baking powder
1/2 t. salt
2 T. sugar
1 egg, beaten

1/2 c. milk
1/2 c. apples, finely chopped
1/2 c. powdered sugar
1 t. cinnamon

Sift dry ingredients together. Combine beaten egg and milk. Gradually blend into dry ingredients. Sir in apples, beat well. Drop by spoonsful onto hot griddle greased with bacon fat. Fry on both sides for 2 minutes or until golden brown. Drain on paper towels. Roll in mixture of powdered sugar and cinnamon.

Christmas Morning Sticky Buns
Donna Alongi

1 pkg. (18-20) frozen roll dough
1 small pkg. butterscotch
    pudding (not instant)
1/2 c. sugar
2 T. cinnamon
1 c. nuts, walnuts or
    pecans (optional)
1 T. melted butter

Before going to bed on Christmas Eve, place frozen roll dough in greased bundt pan. Mix pudding mix, sugar, cinnamon, and nuts (if used). Sprinkle over frozen dough. Pour melted butter over top as evenly as possible. Cover with a towel and leave on counter overnight. In the morning, bake at 350 degrees for 30 minutes, or until lightly brown on top. To serve, invert bundt pan on serving dish. Lift carefully as "sticky sauce" will run out. Yield: 18-20 sticky buns.

140

Buttery Scones

Mary Miner

Serve warm with butter, honey, jam and, of course, your favorite tea!

1 c. buttermilk (skim is fine)
1 egg
2-3 T. sugar
3 1/2 c. unbleached white flour
2 t. baking powder

1 t. baking soda
1/2 t. salt
1/2 c. melted butter
1/2 c. raisins

With electric mixer, beat buttermilk, egg and sugar together. Sift 3 cups of flour with baking powder, soda and salt. Add 2/3 of the flour mixture to the buttermilk mixture and stir well. Gradually add melted butter, stirring well; add remaining flour mixture. Add raisins and a bit more flour if needed. Knead dough on a floured board for 2 to 3 minutes. Cut dough into 3 parts. Form each into a circle and cut into 4 equal quarters. Butter a cookie sheet. Bake at 400 degrees for 20-25 minutes, or until golden brown on top.

Grandma Alta's Pancake Men

Jeffrey Williams

On special occasions or on visits to our grandma's house, she always treats us to a special pancake breakfast. She'll make either a "pancake man" or our own special "initial" pancakes, served with maple syrup. Grandma calls each of us in turn to stand by the stove and watch, while with the spoonful of batter, she makes our special treat.

1 egg, slightly beaten
1 c. milk
2 T. salad oil
1 c. sifted flour

1/2 t. salt
2 t. baking powder
2 T. sugar

Combine egg, milk and oil. Add sifted dry ingredients. Beat until smooth. Heat griddle until hot. Grease griddle. Make pancake men one at a time in the center of the griddle. Fill a serving spoon with batter and pour it in adjoining circles to form torso, head, arms and legs. When bubbles form and burst in batter, turn man with spatula and cook equally long on the other side. Remove to warm plate. Grease griddle again for next man. To make child's initials, simply pour spoonful of pancake batter on hot griddle in the alphabet letter shape of the child's name and cook in same manner. To make a Mickey or teddy bear pancake, pour one large center pancake with two pancake ears attached. Turn over and cook other side. Once on serving plate, make face with fruit, and add whipped cream. Great treat!

✦Festive Food & Drink✦

Sausage Cake
Sandra Curtis

2 eggs
2 1/2 c. brown sugar
1 lb. raisins
2 t. baking soda
1 t. salt

2 t. cinnamon
2 1/2 c. flour
1 c. chopped nuts
1 lb. mild bulk sausage
(uncooked)

Mix eggs, sugar and sausage together. Cook raisins until plump; save one cup water and add to all ingredients. Bake in a greased loaf pan at 350 degrees for 60 minutes. Can be baked in smaller loaf pans, but bake for 35 minutes.

Yummy Breakfast Rolls
Hazel Hayden
Gooseberry Patch Artisan

2 cans crescent rolls
16 oz. cream cheese
1 1/4 c. sugar

1 t. vanilla
1 t. cinnamon
1 stick melted margarine

Unroll 1 can of crescent rolls into the bottom of a 13"x9" pan. Don't press seams together! Mix cheese with 1 cup of sugar and vanilla; spread over rolls. Place second can of rolls over top. Pour melted margarine on and top with mixture of 1/4 cup sugar and cinnamon. Bake for 30 minutes at 350 degrees.

Praline Pecan French Toast
Lisa Englehardt

8 eggs
1 1/2 c. half-and-half
3/4 c. brown sugar plus 1 T.
2 T. vanilla

8 slices french bread (3/4" thick)
1/2 c. butter or oleo
1/2 c. syrup
3/4 c. pecans

Blend eggs, half-and-half, 1 tablespoon brown sugar, and vanilla. Put 1/2 of mixture in 13"x9" baking dish. Add bread, pour rest of mixture over bread. Refrigerate overnight. In another 13"x9" pan, melt butter, add sugar, syrup, and nuts. Place soaked bread over nut mixture. Bake at 350 degrees for 30-35 minutes, until puffed and brown (glass pan works best). Serves 6-8 people.

Overnight Egg Omelet

Carolyn Ritz Lemon

6 oz. box plain croutons
2 c. sharp cheddar cheese, grated
8 eggs
1 t. salt

1 t. prepared mustard
dash of pepper
4 c. milk
crisp crumbled bacon

The evening before, grease a 13"x9" baking pan. Layer croutons, then cheese in the pan. In a bowl, combine eggs, salt, mustard, pepper, and milk. Whip with wire beater and pour over croutons and cheese. Sprinkle bacon on top. Cover and refrigerate overnight. The next morning, bake for 55 minutes at 325 degrees, or until set. Cut into serving pieces.

Gary's Sausage Gravy

Susan Kirschenheiter

1 lb. bulk sausage
4 T. flour

3 c. milk
pepper and salt, to taste

Brown sausage, then drain grease; reserving 3 to 4 tablespoons. Put this grease back into skillet. Add flour and stir. Add milk and the browned sausage. Add pepper and salt, to taste. Cook and stir until hot and blended. Serve on toast or biscuits.

Maple Whipped Butter
1 c. butter
1 1/4 c. maple syrup
1/4 t. plain gelatin
1 t. cold water
Whip butter with an electric mixer until fluffy. Slowly drizzle maple syrup on butter. Soak gelatin in cold water. Then dissolve over hot water. Cool slightly and slowly add to butter. Mix well. Makes 2 cups. Serve on hot toast.

✦Festive Food & Drink✦

Glazed Cinnamon Breakfast Loaf
Kathy Bolyea

1/4 c. brown sugar
1 1/2 t. cinnamon
3 c. biscuit baking mix
1/2 c. sugar

1 c. milk
2 eggs
1/2 c. raisins

Mix brown sugar and cinnamon and reserve. Beat biscuit mix, sugar, milk and eggs. Stir in raisins. Pour 1/3 batter into greased loaf pan. Sprinkle with 3 tablespoons brown sugar mixture. Repeat layers. Bake at 350 degrees for 45 minutes. Pour glaze over top. Makes 1 loaf.

Glaze:

3/4 c. powdered sugar
1 T. softened margarine

3/4 t. vanilla
2/3 t. hot water

Beat all ingredients together.

Gramma's Cornmeal Pancakes
Cindy Graf-Jones

2 eggs
4 c. buttermilk
3/4 c. yellow cornmeal
   (stoneground)
1 3/4 c. flour

1 T. sugar
1 t. salt
1 t. baking soda
1 t. baking powder
2 T. cooking oil

Blend ingredients together well, getting lumps out. Cook on slightly oiled griddle or skillet, on medium heat. Flip when pancakes start to bubble. Optional: Add 1 cup blueberries, just before cooking. Serves 5.

Potato Pancakes
1 egg
1/2 t. salt   1/8 t. pepper
1/4 t. onion juice
2 c. grated raw potato
flour

Beat the egg until light and pale yellow, add the seasonings and the grated potato. Stir in flour, a tablespoon at a time, using only enough to make a thick batter. Drop by spoonfuls into a frying pan containing a little hot shortening and brown slowly on both sides. Serves 6.

Main Feast

⋅Festive Food & Drink⋅

Baked Ham (with Cherry Glaze)

Doris Stegner
Gooseberry Patch

1- 5 lb. canned ham (or any ham)
16 oz. can pitted dark
   sweet cherries
1/4 c. sweet wine

1 T. sugar
1 T. cornstarch
1 T. lemon juice

Bake ham in 325 degree oven for 1 1/2 to 2 hours. After ham has roasted for one hour, make the glaze. Drain cherry liquid into a 1-quart saucepan, stir in sweet wine, sugar, cornstarch and lemon juice. Cook over medium heat stirring until mixture boils and thickens slightly; boil for one minute. During the last 30 minutes of baking, brush ham frequently with some of the cherry sauce. When ham is done, arrange slices on a warm platter. Stir cherries into remaining sauce in saucepan. Heat thoroughly. Spoon some cherry sauce over ham on platter. Serve remaining sauce in a small bowl.

Beef Hash

Donna Crawford

1 T. butter
1/2 c. coarsely chopped onion
1/2 c. coarsely chopped
   green pepper
2 c. of 1/2" diced, peeled
   potatoes
3/4 lb. cooked roast beef,
   diced into 1/2" pieces
14 1/2 oz. can diced, pre-cut
   tomatoes
1 garlic clove, minced
1/2 t. pepper

Melt butter over medium heat in a large skillet or dutch oven. Add onion and green pepper; saute for 3 minutes. Add remaining ingredients and cook until potatoes are tender (about 25 minutes), stirring frequently. Season to taste with salt. Makes two large servings.

Stromboli
Patty Sue Cooper

16 oz. loaf of frozen bread
  dough, thawed
1/4 lb. thinly sliced ham
1/4 lb. sliced pepperoni
3 oz. sliced provolone cheese

1 c. (4 oz.) shredded mozzarella
  cheese
1 T. melted butter or margarine
pizza sauce

Place bread dough on a lightly greased baking sheet; pat to a 15"x10" rectangle. Arrange mozzarella cheese lengthwise down center; layer with pepperoni, then provolone, and ham last. Moisten edges of dough with water. Bring each long edge of dough to center; press edges together securely to seal. Seal ends. Brush loaf with melted butter, and bake at 375 degrees for 20 minutes or until lightly browned. Cool on wire rack. Electric knife works best for slicing. Offer pizza sauce alongside for dipping. Yield depends on how thick you cut, but approximately 12 slices.

Yankee Pleaser Casserole
Beverlee Wallace

2 lbs. bulk sausage, cooked and drained
2 c. grated cheese (longhorn, cheddar, whatever you like)
4 eggs
1 c. cooked grits
1 pkg. (8 1/2 oz.) corn muffin mix
1 3/4 c. hot milk
1/2 c. butter, melted

Grease a 2-quart casserole dish. Layer the sausage and 1 cup of cheese in bottom of casserole. In medium bowl combine the eggs, grits, muffin mix, milk and butter; pour over the sausage and cheese. Top with remaining cheese. At this point, the uncooked mixture may be refrigerated overnight, if desired. Bake at 325 degrees for 1 hour. Should be set in the middle of the oven. Serves 8-10.

> *"Heap on more wood! The wind is chill;*
> *But let it whistle as it will,*
> *We'll keep our Christmas merry still."*
> *Scott Marmion*

✦Festive Food ᵕ Drink✦

Garden Chicken Casserole

Teresa A. German

A nice casserole to take to a buffet or to use up the leftover holiday turkey!

2 c. chicken broth
  (or turkey broth)
2/3 c. sherry (or water)
1 pkg. (6 oz.) long grain and
  wild rice mix
1 can (4 oz.) sliced mushrooms
1 small onion, chopped
2 small carrots, grated
1 small green pepper, chopped

1/4 c. butter or margarine
3 c. diced cooked chicken
  (or turkey)
1 pkg. (8 oz.) cream cheese
2 c. (8 oz.) shredded American
  cheese
1 c. evaporated milk
1/3 c. grated parmesan cheese
1/2 c. sliced almonds

In medium saucepan, bring broth and 1/3 cup sherry (water) to a boil. Add rice mix, cover and simmer on low heat 25-30 minutes, or until all liquid is absorbed. Preheat oven to 350 degrees. In a dutch oven saute onions, carrots, and green pepper in butter or margarine until tender (about 5 minutes). Add rice, chicken (turkey) and mushrooms; mix well. Place cream cheese, American cheese and milk in a saucepan and melt over medium heat, stirring until smooth. Add to mixture in dutch oven and add remaining sherry (water); mix thoroughly. Pour into a greased 13"x9"x2" casserole dish. Top with parmesan cheese and almonds. Cover and bake for 35 minutes; uncover and bake 15 minutes longer, or until bubbly. Yields: about 8 servings. This can be made a day ahead and refrigerated overnight. You will need to increase your baking time to 45 minutes covered and 15 minutes uncovered. You can garnish if you like, make raw carrot flowers with green onion stem and petals.

Baked Chicken Casserole

Janet Schaeper
(Vickie's sister)

1 lb. cooked cut up chicken
1/2 c. diced celery
1/4 c. diced pimiento
10 oz. frozen peas
1/4 c. diced green pepper
1/4 c. diced onion

1 1/2 c. mayonnaise
1 1/2 T. lemon juice
salt and pepper to taste
1 c. grated cheese
  (American or colby)
1 c. bread crumbs

Mix first five ingredients, add next three and pour into a greased casserole and bake at 375 degrees for 20 minutes. Top with cheese and bread crumbs mixed and bake an additional 20 minutes or until the cheese bubbles.

Chicken Breasts with Champagne Sauce
Kathy Bolyea

4 boneless chicken breasts
2 T. margarine
1/2 c. fresh mushrooms

1/3 c. champagne
1/3 c. sour cream

Heat margarine and add chicken. Brown on both sides. Remove chicken to a baking dish. Saute mushrooms and set aside. Stir champagne into drippings. Simmer until well heated. Pour over chicken, cover and bake at 350 degrees for 20 minutes. Remove chicken to platter, reserve liquid. Add sour cream and salt and pepper, to taste, to the reserved liquid. Whisk until smooth. Pour over chicken and top with mushrooms. Serves 4.

Christmas Meatloaf
Debbi Kinsey

Super simple! Make this during that hectic week of Christmas. Put it together the night before a very busy day, then all you have to do is pop it in the oven.

1 lb. ground beef
1 c. Italian bread crumbs
1 egg
2 T. minced onion
1/4 c. chopped celery
1/4 c. grated carrot
1/4 c. chopped green pepper

1/2 of 16 oz. can Italian stewed
   tomatoes, drained
1 t. dry mustard
1/2 t. oregano
1/2 t. salt
1/2 t. black pepper

Combine all ingredients and place in a greased 9" loaf pan. Bake at 350 degrees for 1 hour.

Christmas Night Turkey Casserole
Carol Weiss

2 c. diced turkey
1 can (4 oz.) mushroom pieces
1 c. uncooked instant rice
   (cooked in 2 c. of broth)
1 can undiluted mushroom soup

1 c. diced celery
3/4 c. mayonnaise
1 c. cornflakes
3 T. butter or margarine, melted
1/4 to 1/2 c. slivered almonds

Mix together in a 2-quart greased casserole all of the above, except cornflakes, margarine or butter and almonds. Mix cornflakes with melted margarine or butter, and almonds. Spread on top; bake for 40 minutes at 350 degrees uncovered. Serves 6-8.

·Festive Food & Drink·

Chicken Divine

Paul Gaulke
Gooseberry Patch

4- 5 oz. cans chicken breast or
    5-6 boneless chicken breasts
1 (20 oz.) large family size
    bag broccoli
2 cans cream of chicken soup
8-10 oz. mayonnaise

3 c. shredded cheddar cheese
cornflake crumbs
    (approximately 1 1/2 c.)
margarine
curry powder (mild or hot)

Lay cooked broccoli in the bottom of a 15"x9" glass casserole dish. Place chicken (all 4 cans) on top of the broccoli. In a mixing bowl combine cream of chicken, mayonnaise and curry powder (to taste); stir. Spread mixture on top of chicken and broccoli. Layer top with shredded cheese. Melt margarine (enough to moisten cornflake crumbs when added). Add cornflake crumbs; mix. Spread on top of the casserole. Place in 350 degree oven and bake for 45 minutes or until cornflake crumbs brown slightly. Remove from oven and serve. Serves 6-8 generous portions.

Meatballs and Sauerkraut

Susan Kirschenheiter

sauerkraut
2 slices wet bread, squeezed well and torn into small pieces
1 1/2 lb. ground chuck (or meat loaf mix of ground beef and
    ground pork)
1/4 c. regular rice (soaked in hot
    water for 1/2 hour)
2 eggs
1 small onion, diced
salt and pepper (to taste)

Put as much sauerkraut in the bottom of a baking dish as you would need to serve your family. Mix remaining ingredients well and shape into meatballs, place them on top of the sauerkraut and bake at 350 degrees for 1 to 1 1/2 hours, or until meatballs are done to your liking. Serve with mashed potatoes for the main meal.

Easiest Lasagna

Diane Dollak

30 oz. prepared spaghetti sauce
1 1/2 c. water
1 lb. dry lasagna noodles
1 lb. shredded mozzarella cheese

1 lb. ricotta cheese
parmesan cheese

Combine spaghetti sauce and water. Layer in a 13"x9" baking pan:

1 cup sauce, 1/3 dry noodles, half of the mozzarella, half of the ricotta; another cup of sauce, another 1/3 noodles, rest of mozzarella, rest of ricotta; another cup of sauce, rest of noodles, rest of sauce; top with parmesan. Cover tightly with aluminium foil and bake at 350 degrees for 1 hour. This amount is great for a party, or you can make it in two 8"x8" or 9"x9" pans and freeze one for a wintry night. The entire recipe makes about 12 servings.

Chicken Cheese Bake

Linda Tittle

6 chicken breast halves, skinned
and boned
6 slices Swiss cheese
1/4 lb. sliced fresh mushrooms
(optional)
1/2 c. white wine

1/2 stick butter, melted
10 3/4 oz. can cream of
chicken soup
2 c. herb-seasoned
stuffing mix

Place chicken in a slightly greased 13"x9" baking dish. Top each chicken piece with cheese, lay sliced mushrooms on top of cheese. Mix soup with wine and pour on top. Spread on stuffing mix and drizzle butter over top. Bake at 350 degrees for 45-50 minutes. Serves 5-6

Roast in Wine

Georgene Kornreich
Gooseberry Patch Artisan

5 or 6 lb. chuck roast
1 pkg. Italian dressing
1 can beef consomme

1 lb. fresh sliced mushrooms
1 large onion, sliced
3 c. cream sherry

Make deep cuts on top of beef. Rub with dry salad dressing mix. Stuff slits with mushrooms and onions. Pile what is left on top of roast. Combine sherry and beef consomme. Pour over top of roast. Cover and let set overnight. Bake at 400 degrees for 1 hour; turn heat down to 250 degrees, and bake 4 to 5 hours. Serve with oven roasted potatoes.

♦Festive Food & Drink♦

Pot Roast Special

David Bamford
(JoAnn's Dad)

5 lb. top, bottom or rump roast
enough olive oil to
    cover bottom of pan
1 large chopped onion
6-8 cloves garlic, chopped
1 stalk celery, chopped
1 T. rosemary
2 T. parsley

1 T. black pepper
1 t. basil
2 cans beef broth
2 cans cream of mushroom soup
2 c. hearty Burgundy wine
6 medium potatoes
8 carrots

Saute onions and celery in olive oil in a large heavy pot. Brown roast on all sides. Add broth, soup and seasonings; let simmer for about 2 1/2 to 3 hours. Produces complete dinner with plenty of rich gravy.

The Famed Liz
Martin's Marvelous Minestrone

Joanne Martin-Robinson
Gooseberry Patch

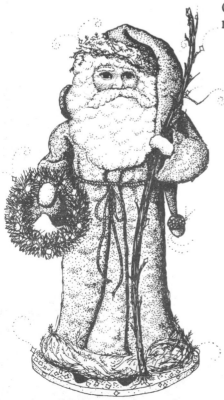

Great with salad and crusty bread. Best if made a day ahead.

1 lb. ground beef
1 c. onions, chopped
1 c. potatoes, chopped
1 c. carrots, chopped
1/2 c. celery, diced
1 large (28-32 oz.) can tomatoes
1/4 c. uncooked rice
1 small bay leaf
1/2 t. thyme
1 to 2 t. salt
1/4 t. basil
1/8 t. pepper
1 qt. water
grated cheese

Cook meat with onion until brown. Add potatoes, carrots, celery, tomatoes and water. Bring to a boil and add spices. Cover and simmer for one hour or until the vegetables are tender. About one-half hour before serving, add the rice. Serve with grated cheese on top.

Sensational Sides

·Festive Food & Drink·

Cranberry Cups

Jane Lusk

1 can jellied
    cranberry sauce
1 small can crushed
    pineapple, drained
3 T. lemon juice

1 c. heavy whipping cream
3 oz. pkg. cream cheese, softened
1/4 c. (or less) mayonnaise
1/2 c. powdered sugar
1 c. chopped pecans or walnuts

Mix together cranberry sauce, pineapple and lemon juice in a small bowl and set aside. Whip cream, add remaining ingredients, leaving the nuts until last. Fold in nuts. Using 5-ounce paper cups, layer the 2 mixtures starting with the cranberry, then cream, etc., ending with cream mix. Freeze. A muffin tin works well to hold the cups. To serve, peel off paper cup and invert onto plate. Can be topped with whipped cream and a cherry. Serves 8. You can make them smaller by using 3-ounce paper cups, which would yield more.

Frozen Lime Mint Salad

Jackie Hoover

8 1/2 oz. can crushed pineapple,
    undrained
20 oz. can crushed pineapple,
    undrained
3 oz. pkg. lime gelatin
7 oz. jar marshmallow cream
1 c. butter mints, coarsely chopped
8 oz. carton whipped topping, thawed

In a large bowl combine pineapple, gelatin, marshmallow cream and butter mints. Fold in whipped topping. Spoon into muffin liners in muffin tins. Cover and freeze for 6 hours or overnight. Peel off paper and serve immediately on a lettuce leaf. This makes at least 18 regular-sized "muffins". I usually make as many as I wish to use for a luncheon or party and freeze the extras in a large container.

154

Sensational Sides

Rice Pudding
Sharon Darling

This recipe was my great-grandmother's. It's always been a holiday favorite for us.

raisins, as many as you want
1/2 c. long grain rice
dash of salt
1 c. water
1/2 stick butter or margarine

4 c. milk
1/2 c. sugar
1 t. vanilla
2 eggs, room temperature

Soak raisins in a dish of water while preparing pudding. In a large pot combine and cook rice, salt and water until it starts to thicken. Add butter or margarine and stir (mixture will turn yellow). Add milk and cook until thick, approximately 1 hour, stirring occasionally. When thickened, slowly add the sugar. Remove from flame, and add the vanilla. Beat the two eggs and slowly pour them into the pudding. Drain raisins and add to pudding mixture. Heat a few minutes until bubbly/thick. Let cool. Serve warm or refrigerate for cold pudding. Store in the refrigerator.

Cranberry Candles
Juanita Williams

2- 1 lb. cans whole
    cranberry sauce
1 1/2 c. boiling water
3 oz. pkg. cherry-flavored
    gelatin

1/4 t. salt
1 T. lemon juice
1/2 c. mayonnaise
1 orange, peeled and diced
1/4 c. walnuts, chopped

Plan for candles by collecting twelve (6 oz.) empty fruit juice cans, in advance. Heat cranberry sauce; strain and set berries aside. Combine hot juice and water; add gelatin, stirring until dissolved. Add salt and lemon juice. Cool; place in refrigerator until thickened enough to mound slightly when dropped from a spoon. Beat in mayonnaise with rotary beater until light and fluffy. Fold in cranberries, fruit and nuts. Divide mixture evenly into the fruit juice cans. Chill 4 hours or longer. Unmold on Christmas doilies. To flame, insert small wax birthday candles into tops of cranberry candles and light. So festive!

"Christmas is coming, the geese are getting fat . . ."
Unknown

Festive Food & Drink

Sweet Potato Pudding

Donna Shadel

3 eggs
1/2 c. brown sugar
1/2 c. butter, melted
1/4 t. salt
1 t. vanilla

12 oz. can evaporated milk
1/2 c. coconut
1 can sweet potatoes
marshmallows

Mash sweet potatoes. Beat eggs; add brown sugar, melted butter, salt, vanilla, milk and coconut. Add to mashed potatoes. Pour into a 2-quart casserole and bake at 350 degrees for 50 minutes, or until knife in center shows that it is set. Top with marshmallows and place under broiler until brown on top.

Hardy 3-Bean Bake

Linda Zell

5 slices of bacon, cut into 1" pieces
2 large onions, cut in rings and
    then in half
3/4 t. dry mustard
1/4 c. white vinegar
1/2 c. brown sugar
16 oz. can green lima beans,
    drained and rinsed
16 oz. can light red kidney beans,
    drained and rinsed
28 oz. can pork and beans
    (don't drain)

Put bacon and onions in a large frying pan. Fry just until the bacon is done, not crisp (do not drain). Add mustard, vinegar, and brown sugar. Simmer until the sugar dissolves. Add the three kinds of beans and combine well. Put into a 2-quart casserole, cover and bake at 350 degrees for 45 minutes. Serves 12-15.

156

Sensational Sides

Sweet Potato Casserole

Barbara Anderson

3 c. mashed sweet potatoes
1 c. granulated sugar
2 eggs

1 t. vanilla
1/2 c. margarine, melted

Mix ingredients together and pour into a buttered casserole. Add topping.

Topping:

1 c. packed brown sugar
1/3 c. flour

1 c. finely chopped pecans

Mix together flour and sugar with fork and sprinkle crumbs on top of casserole. Cover with finely chopped pecans, then dot with butter. Bake at 350 degrees for 30 minutes.

Baked Potatoes and Broccoli

Sharon Hall
Gooseberry Patch

6-8 baking potatoes
1 small bag of frozen broccoli
1 T. margarine
1/2 lb. bacon
shredded cheese (your favorite)

Bake potatoes and cut them in half. Scrape out potato centers, put in a bowl and mash. Add margarine. Cook broccoli according to package instructions; drain and mash. Add broccoli to potato mixture, mix well. Fry bacon until crisp, drain. Crumble bacon, add to potato and broccoli mixture. Refill potato skins with mixture. Place in microwave for 2 minutes. Sprinkle shredded cheese over potatoes.

Festive Food & Drink

Broccoli Cheese Casserole

Paula Acklin

1/3 c. melted butter
1 t. salt
1 c. sharp cheddar cheese, grated
1 large egg, beaten
1 c. milk

1 c. cooked rice
10 oz. package of frozen
   chopped broccoli,
   cooked
1 small onion, diced

Preheat oven to 350 degrees. Mix butter, salt, cheese, egg, milk, and onion. Blend with rice, add broccoli and pour into buttered casserole dish. Bake for 1 hour. Serves 6.

Holiday Potatoes

Susan A. Harvey

4 lbs. white potatoes
   (baked or boiled)
1 c. chopped onion
1/4 c. butter
1 can cream of celery soup

1 pt. sour cream
1 1/2 c. shredded cheddar
   cheese
1/2 c. crushed cornflakes
3 T. melted butter

Remove skin from potatoes and shred into bowl. Saute onions, remove from heat. Stir in soup, sour cream and cheese. Pour mixture over potatoes and mix well. Turn into greased 13"x9" pan. Cover and refrigerate overnight. Sprinkle with cornflakes and drizzle with butter. Bake at 350 degrees for 1 hour.

Zucchini Dressing Casserole

Annie Wolfe
Gooseberry Patch

6 c. diced, unpeeled zucchini
1/4 c. diced onions
3/4 stick of margarine
8 oz. pkg. herb-seasoned
   stuffing mix

1 c. sour cream
1 c. cream of chicken soup
1 c. grated carrots

Boil zucchini, onions and carrots for 5 minutes; drain well. Melt margarine and mix with stuffing mix. Mix together sour cream and soup; fold in zucchini, onions and carrots. Put 1/2 of stuffing mix in a 13"x9" baking dish. Pour the zucchini mixture over the stuffing mix and top with the remaining stuffing mix. Bake at 350 degrees for 35 minutes. Serve hot. Makes 12-15 servings.

Sensational Sides

Sage Dressing
Linda Arndt

3/4 c. onions, minced
1 1/2 c. celery, minced
1 c. margarine
9 c. bread cubes
1 t. salt (optional)
1 1/2 t. sage

1 t. thyme
1/2 t. rosemary
1/2 t. pepper
2 beaten eggs
2 c. chicken bouillion

Saute onions and celery in margarine. Stir in 1/3 of bread cubes. Turn into deep bowl and add remaining ingredients. Bake at 350 degrees for 1 hour in a 13"x9" glass pan or small roasting pan. Yield: 9 cups of stuffing.

Christmas Eve Salad
Georgene Kornreich
Gooseberry Patch
Artisan

1/4 c. chopped almonds
1 T. plus 1 t. sugar
any kind of fruit (sliced
    strawberries, kiwi,
    apples, etc.)
1/4 head iceberg lettuce
1/4 head romaine lettuce
2 stalks celery, sliced thin
5 green onions, sliced
1 can mandarin oranges

Cook almonds in sugar on low heat until sugar melts. Cool on waxed paper; break apart. Combine all ingredients.

Dressing:

2 T. sugar
2 T. vinegar
1/2 t. salt
dash of pepper
1/4 c. vegetable oil
1 T. chopped fresh parsley

Mix all ingredients together.

✦Festive Food & Drink✦

Spiced Cranberry-Orange Mold

Lois Eisenhut

12 oz. cranberries
1/2 c. sugar
2 pkgs. (4-serving size) or 1
   pkg. (8-serving size)
   orange or lemon gelatin
1 1/2 c. boiling water

1 c. cold water
1 T. lemon juice
1/4 t. ground cinnamon
1/8 t. ground cloves
1 orange, sectioned and diced
1/2 c. chopped walnuts

Place cranberries in blender or food processor; cover. Process until finely chopped; mix with sugar and set aside. Dissolve gelatin in boiling water; add cold water, lemon juice and spices. Refrigerate until slightly thickened. Fold in cranberry mixture, orange sections and walnuts. Spoon into 5-cup mold; refrigerate until firm (about 4 hours). Unmold. Garnish with orange slices, lemon slices and cranberries, if desired. Note: 1 can (16 ounces) whole berry cranberry sauce may be substituted for fresh cranberries. Omit sugar and reduce cold water to 1/2 cup. Makes 10 servings.

Hash Brown Potato Casserole

Linda J. Tittle

2 lbs. hash brown potatoes
1/2 c. butter
1 can cream of mushroom
   soup
1 pt. sour cream

1/4 c. chopped onion
1/2 c. shredded cheddar cheese
   (or pasteurized processed
   cheese spread)

Heat butter with soup. Blend in the rest of the ingredients. Stir in thawed potatoes. Place in a 2 1/2-quart buttered casserole. Bake at 350 degrees for 45 minutes to 1 hour. Makes 10-12 servings.

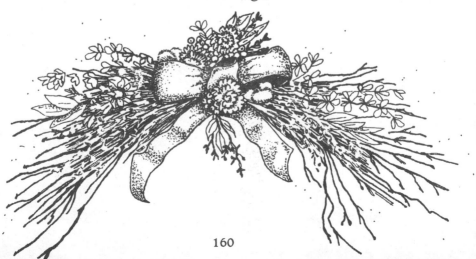

Sensational Sides

Broccoli Curry

Jane Lusk

1 bunch broccoli
1/2 t. salt
1 can cream of chicken soup
1/2 c. mayonnaise

1/4 t. curry powder
2 T. lemon juice
1/2 c. stale bread crumbs
2 T. melted butter

Cut broccoli into stalks (not chopped pieces); cook in salted water, just until tender. Arrange drained broccoli in a greased 2-quart casserole. In a small bowl combine soup, mayonnaise and curry. Sprinkle the lemon juice over broccoli, then spread soup mixture over broccoli. Top with bread crumbs and drizzle with melted butter. Bake at 350 degrees for 20 minutes. Serves 6.

Christmas Buffet Potato Salad

Georgene Kornreich
Gooseberry Patch Artisan

5 lbs. potatoes, boiled
1/2 c. white vinegar
1 large onion, chopped
4-5 stalks celery, chopped
6 hard boiled eggs, sliced

1 small green pepper, chopped
1 t. dill seed or dill weed
2 c. mayonnaise
small container sour cream

After potatoes have been boiled, slice them while still warm. Pour 1/4 cup of vinegar over potatoes; add onion, celery, boiled eggs and pepper. Add dill seed or dill weed. In a bowl mix together mayonnaise, sour cream, and the other 1/4 cup of vinegar; pour over potatoes. Season with salt and pepper to taste. This is best if made the day before. Yield: 12-15 servings.

Nanny Schantz's Turkey Dressing

Phyllis Ann Schantz

1 loaf white bread, broken up
2 large onions, chopped
1 stick butter
3 stalks of celery, chopped
2 eggs

1 c. applesauce
fresh parsley
3 t. allspice
3 t. thyme, more if desired
salt and pepper to taste

Chop onions and saute in the butter until tender. Soak the bread in water and squeeze out all the water; place in a bowl. Add the sauted onions and all of the other ingredients; mix together well. Stuff your turkey and enjoy a very tasty old-fashioned dressing.

Festive Food & Drink

Country Dressing
Denise Castle

This makes a good side dish or a great main dish for those turkey leftovers. Especially good with gravy!

1 large loaf bread, toasted and cubed
1 c. carrots
1 c. potatoes
3/4 c. finely chopped celery
2 to 3 c. cooked chicken or turkey, chopped

1 to 2 c. broth (chicken or turkey, use milk to make 2 c., if needed)
1 onion, chopped
7 eggs
1/4 c. butter
salt and pepper to taste

Prepare toasted bread cubes. Cut up carrots, potatoes and celery; cook and drain. Combine all ingredients except butter. Cut butter in pieces and put on top before baking. Place in a 13"x9" pan and cook at 350 degrees for 1 hour, or until lightly browned. Serves 8-10.

Swedish Green Potatoes
Nancy Campbell

1 pkg. frozen chopped spinach
4 large potatoes (about 3 lbs.)
3/4 c. undiluted evaporated milk
1 t. sugar
1/4 lb. margarine

1 t. salt
1/4 t. pepper
2 T. chopped chives
1 1/2 t. dried dill weed

Cook frozen spinach in as little water as possible; drain well. Boil potatoes, cook 20 minutes (or until done), and mash thoroughly. Add margarine, sugar, salt, pepper and milk; beat until light and fluffy with electric mixer. Add chives, dill weed and spinach; beat again. Turn into a well buttered 1 1/2-quart casserole. Bake at 350 degrees for 20 minutes, or until thoroughly heated. May be made ahead of time. Yield: 8 servings.

Great nostalgic Christmas videos you won't want to miss this holiday season are "White Christmas," "Miracle on 34th Street," "The Honeymooners' Christmas," "It's a Wonderful Life," "Meet Me in St. Louis," "A Christmas Carol," "The Judy Garland Christmas Show," "Ed Sullivan's Classic Christmas," and "The Apartment."

Sensational Sides

Onion Kuchen
Kara Kimerline

2 medium onions; peeled, sliced
    and separated into rings
3 T. butter
1 pkg. refrigerator biscuits

1 egg
1 c. (8 oz.) sour cream
1/2 t. salt
1 t. poppy seeds

Saute onions slowly in butter until soft. Separate 10 biscuits; place in a single layer in an ungreased 8" layer cake pan. Press together to cover bottom completely. Spoon onion mixture on top. Beat egg slightly in a small bowl; blend in salt and sour cream. Spoon over onion mixture; sprinkle with poppy seeds. Bake in 375 degree oven for 30 minutes, or until topping is set. Slice into wedges; serve warm. Serves 8.

Curry Spinach Tortellini
Jacqueline Lash-Idler

16 oz. pkg. frozen
    cheese tortellini
10 oz. pkg. frozen spinach
2 c. half-and-half
3 T. flour

1/2 c. butter
2 T. curry powder
1/2 t. salt
1/2 t. pepper

Boil and drain tortellini; then spinach. Press water out of spinach. Melt butter in a saucepan. Whisk in flour, beating constantly, until flour dissolves. Add half-and-half, curry, salt and pepper. On low flame, whisk until thickened. Fold in spinach. Toss with hot tortellini. Serve immediately or keep warm on a hot plate, or in a crockpot set to low (add milk should it dry out).

Pickled Beet Eggs
Sonia Bracamonte

1 doz. hard boiled eggs, peeled
2 c. beet juice
3/4 c. vinegar cider
2 c. water
dash allspice
dash cloves and cinnamon

After mixing ingredients, place peeled eggs in container of juice to thoroughly cover eggs. Stir often at first, so all of the eggs dye evenly. Leave overnight and serve the following day for best results.

❧ Festive Food & Drink ❧

Cranberry Salad Delight
Sue Daugherty

2- 3 oz. pkgs. raspberry gelatin
3 oz. pkg. orange gelatin
20 oz. can crushed pineapple,
   drained (save juice)
16 oz. can whole cranberry sauce
2 stalks of celery, chopped
1 peeled apple, chopped

11 oz. can mandarin oranges,
   drained (save juice)
1/2 c. chopped walnuts
8 oz. cream cheese, softened
2 T. salad dressing
1/2 pkg. dry whipped topping
   mix

Dissolve gelatins in 2 cups of boiling water. Measure juice in measuring cup, should have 3 cups, if not, add water to make right amount. Add this to already dissolved gelatin; place in the refrigerator to partially set. Fold in the rest of ingredients until evenly distributed in gelatin. Chill for several hours. Makes 2 salads. Note: Buy cranberries when they are on sale and freeze them. Cranberries have a better flavor after being frozen...and you save on cost too!

Spiced Peaches
Sarah Bennett
Gooseberry Patch Artisan

Arranged on a platter with sprigs of parsley or watercress, these peaches make a beautiful and tasty garnish!

1 can (1 lb.13 oz.) peach halves
   in heavy syrup, drained
1/3 c. granulated sugar
2 c. liquid (peach syrup plus
   water)
2 T. white vinegar

24 whole cloves
6 allspice berries
3- 1" cinnamon sticks
1/8 t. salt
cranberry-orange relish,
   as needed

Place well drained peach halves, flat side up in a glass loaf pan. Combine sugar, liquid, vinegar, spices and salt in saucepan. Bring to a boil; reduce heat and simmer for 10 minutes. Pour hot syrup (and spices) over peaches. Let peaches stand in syrup until cold. Refrigerate for several hours. When ready to use, drain peaches and fill centers with cranberry-orange relish.

*"Most all the time, the whole year round, there ain't no flies on me,
But jest 'fore Christmas, I'm as good as I kin be!"*
Eugene Field

Sensational Sides

Eggnog Fruit Salad

Deborah Hilton

1 c. chilled eggnog
1 envelope dry whipped
   topping mix
1/4 t. freshly grated nutmeg
16 oz. can sliced peaches,
   drained
13 oz. can pineapple tidbits,
   drained

medium unpared apple, chopped
1/4 c. drained and halved
   maraschino cherries
1/2 c. fresh or frozen blueberries
1/2 c. walnuts, chopped

In a small bowl, combine eggnog, topping mix and nutmeg. Beat at high speed with electric mixer, until soft peaks form (about 5 minutes). Combine fruits and nuts. Fold into eggnog mixture. Cover and chill in refrigerator for several hours, or overnight. Stir gently before serving.
Yield: 6-8 servings.

Apricot Mold

Mariann Smith

2- 3 oz. pkgs. apricot gelatin
1 1/2 c. boiling water
2 T. sugar
8 oz. pkg. cream cheese
small can mandarin oranges,
   undrained
small can crushed pineapple,
   undrained
1 box (2 envelopes) dry
   whipped topping mix

Dissolve gelatin in boiling water and add sugar. Cut in chunks of cream cheese and beat together with electric mixer. Place mixture in refrigerator and when it starts to gel, fold in fruit and whipped topping mix. Put mixture into a 2-quart mold and set in refrigerator until solid. Serves 8-12.

✦Festive Food & Drink✦

Raspberry Salad Wreath

Hazel Hayden
Gooseberry Patch Artisan

1 large pkg. raspberry gelatin
3 1/2 c. boiling water
10 oz. pkg. frozen raspberries
1 t. lemon juice
8 oz. pkg. cream cheese
1/4 c. chopped nuts

Dissolve gelatin in hot water. Add thawed raspberries, juice and lemon juice. Let partially set. Roll cream cheese into 16 cheese balls; roll balls in chopped nuts, and line the bottom of ring mold. Add gelatin and refrigerate. Unmold onto plate and serve with whipped cream or mayonnaise.

Christmas Fruit Salad

Gina Adams

2- 10 oz. pkgs. of strawberries, frozen
1 c. boiling water
2 small pkgs. strawberry gelatin
1 lb. crushed pineapple, drained
2 medium bananas, mashed
1 pt. sour cream

Dissolve gelatin in water. Add strawberries, pineapple and bananas. Pour 1/2 of mixture in mold. Let set 30 minutes. Top with sour cream; then pour on remaining mixture. Let set for 2 hours. It's a good idea to make this a day early.

Hot Chicken Salad

Rosalie Sporrer

2 c. diced cooked chicken or turkey
1 c. chopped diced celery
1/4 c. slivered almonds (optional)
2 or 3 T. lemon juice
1 T. chopped onion
1/4 c. mayonnaise
1 can cream of chicken soup

Mix together in a 9"x9" baking dish; top with shredded cheddar cheese and crushed potato chips (your judgment on amounts). Bake at 350 degrees until bubbly hot (about 30 minutes). Serves 4.

Teens can be particularly hard to buy for. Here are some great ideas...CD's, cassettes, gift certificates for videos, video game rentals, arcades or bookstores, sporting goods, magazine subscriptions, movie passes, blank cassettes, concert tickets, batteries and art supplies.

Festive Food & Drink

Peanut Butter Cake

Kathy Bolyea

1 c. milk
2 T. margarine
2 c. flour
2 c. sugar
1 t. baking powder

4 eggs
1 t. vanilla
1 small jar peanut butter
6 chocolate candy bars

Scald the milk and margarine. Then add flour, sugar, baking powder, eggs and vanilla. Spray edged jelly roll pan with cooking spray. Pour batter into pan. Bake at 350 degrees for 20 minutes until edges turn brown (may not look brown on top). Spread peanut butter on hot cake. Melt candy bars and spread on top of peanut butter. Cool slightly and then refrigerate until firm. Cut into small pieces.

Gumdrop Cookies

Lois Dick

4 eggs
1 T. cold water
2 c. light brown sugar
2 c. flour
1/2 t. salt
1 t. cinnamon
1/2 c. pecans, dredged in flour
1 c. shredded gumdrops,
    dredged in flour

Beat eggs together, add water; beat in brown sugar. Beat well. Sift flour, salt and cinnamon; add to egg mixture. Fold in gumdrops and pecans. Bake in a large flat greased pan for 30 minutes in a 325 degree oven. Frost while still warm.

Frosting:

3 T. butter or margarine
1 t. orange rind
2 t. orange juice
powdered sugar (enough to
    make frosting spreadable)

Mix all ingredients;
frost and cut in long bars.

Millionaire Brownies

Jean Shaffer

8 oz. pkg. cream cheese, divided
1 1/2 c. sugar, divided
1 c. plus 2 T. flour, divided
1 c. softened butter or margarine, divided
3 eggs, divided
2 1/2 t. vanilla, divided
3 c. confectioner's sugar

2- 1 oz. squares unsweetened chocolate, divided
1 1/4 c. chopped walnuts, divided
1 t. baking powder
1 c. semi-sweet chocolate chips
2 c. miniature marshmallows
1/4 c. milk

In small mixing bowl, blend 6 ounces of cream cheese, 1/2 cup of sugar, 2 tablespoons flour, 1/4 cup butter, 1 egg, and 1/2 teaspoon vanilla; set aside. In a medium saucepan, over medium heat, melt 1 square of chocolate and 1/2 cup of butter. Remove from heat; add 1 cup sugar, 1 cup flour, 1 cup nuts, baking powder, 1 teaspoon vanilla, and 2 eggs; blend well. Spray 13"x9"x2" pan with non-stick spray; spread batter in pan. Spread cream cheese mixture over batter. In a small bowl combine 1/4 cup nuts and chocolate chips; sprinkle over cheese layer. Bake at 350 degrees for 28 minutes (almost done). Sprinkle marshmallows on top; return to oven for 2 minutes. In medium saucepan, melt 1/4 cup butter, 1 square of chocolate, 2 ounces cream cheese and milk. Remove from heat; stir in confectioner's sugar and 1 teaspoon of vanilla. Immediately drizzle over marshmallows. Chill well, cut into bars. Yield: 30.

Holiday Cranberry Cobbler

Judy Roque

1 pkg. yellow cake mix
1/2 t. cinnamon
1/4 t. nutmeg
2 sticks butter, softened

1/2 c. chopped pecans
21 oz. can peach pie filling
16 oz. can whole cranberry sauce
vanilla ice cream

Preheat oven to 350 degrees. Combine dry cake mix, cinnamon and nutmeg in a bowl. Cut in butter with pastry blender until crumbly. Stir in nuts, set aside. Combine peach pie filling and cranberry sauce in ungreased 13"x9"x2" pan. Mix well. Sprinkle crumb mixture over fruit. Bake 45-50 minutes, or until golden brown. Serve warm with ice cream.

Creme de Menthe Squares

Jackie Samo

For gift giving, wrap squares individually in plastic wrap, fill clear glass jars and decorate with ribbons.

1 1/4 c. butter or margarine (I use margarine)
1/2 c. unsweetened cocoa powder
3 1/2 c. powdered sugar
1 egg, beaten
1 t. vanilla
2 c. graham cracker crumbs
1/3 c. green creme de menthe
    (syrup can be used)
1 1/2 c. semi-sweet chocolate chips

Bottom Layer:

In a saucepan combine 1/2 cup butter and cocoa powder. Heat and stir until well blended. Remove from heat and add 1/2 of the powdered sugar, egg and vanilla. Stir in graham cracker crumbs, mix well. Press into bottom of ungreased 13"x9" pan.

Middle Layer:

Melt another 1/2 c. butter. In a small mixer bowl combine melted butter and creme de menthe. At low speed, beat in the remaining 3 cups powdered sugar until smooth. Spread over chocolate layer. Chill.

Top Layer:

Melt the remaining 1/4 cup of butter and the chocolate chips. Spread over mint layer. Chill slightly. Cut into small squares; store in refrigerator. Squares can be made well ahead of time and frozen. Yields 96 small squares.

Candy Strawberries

Jackie Hoover

These are beautiful for a holiday tea party and great for a cookie exchange as they are a pretty addition to any tray of cookies.

6 oz. strawberry gelatin	1/2 t. vanilla
1 c. ground pecans or walnuts	red sugar crystals
1 c. ground coconut	green food coloring
3/4 c. sweetened condensed milk	slivered almonds

Mix together gelatin, nuts, coconut, condensed milk and vanilla. Shape mixture into "strawberries". Chill for 1 hour. Roll chilled berries in red sugar crystals. Mix green food coloring and a little water in a small dish. Briefly stir slivered almonds in mixture to tint green. Dry on paper towels (you may let dry overnight). Use green tinted almonds as stems for berries. Store in a cool place.

Death By Chocolate

Wendy Lee Paffenroth

Sinfully good, but don't ever tell if you go for seconds or sneak a taste at 2 a.m.!

1 chocolate cake mix
1 large tub of whipped topping (vanilla or chocolate)
1 5.9 oz. box of instant chocolate pudding
2 large chocolate coated toffee or krispy rice candy bars

Bake cake in a 13"x9" baking dish or bundt pan. Cool. Thaw whipped topping. Prepare pudding. In a large glass bowl (I use a clear plastic tub), break up a few pieces of cake on the bottom. Spoon some whipped topping over it, then a few spoonsful of pudding, crumbled candy bars and repeat layers. I like to finish with the whipped topping and sprinkle chocolate jimmies on the top. Let sit in refrigerator at least 4 hours. Spoon it out onto small plates. It looks like a mess, but my kids prefer it on birthdays to a cake!

Fill a van (or more than one) with plenty of warm blankets, great food and lots of good friends. Open the windows, play Christmas carols and wish all a "Merry Christmas!" A happy ending would be a tailgate party with mugs of hot cocoa and Christmas cookies.

✦Festive Food & Drink✦

Lollipop Cookies
Margo Jackson

1 pkg. moist cake mix
3/4 c. water

2 eggs
20-24 wooden popsicle sticks

Preheat oven to 375 degrees. Beat cake mix (dry), water, and eggs in a large mixing bowl on low speed for 30 seconds; then on high speed for 2 minutes. Drop dough by rounded tablespoonsful 3" apart on a greased cookie sheet. Insert wooden stick 1 1/2" into edge of dough. Bake 8-11 minutes or until puffed and almost no indentation remains when touched. Cool for 1 minute. Remove from cookie sheet; cool on wire rack; frost and decorate.

Variation #1:

Omit the stick and make them into sandwich cookies.

Variation #2:

Use a chocolate chip dough without nuts or chips. Insert the wooden stick into one half of a small fun-sized chocolate candy bar; cover bar with dough and bake. Now you have a cookie-candy lollipop.

Gram's Lemon Sugar Cookies
Pat Akers

I've made these cookies every year for the last 35 years. They have become a family tradition at our house and it "just ain't Christmas without them!"

1 1/2 c. sugar
1/2 c. butter
1/2 c. vegetable shortening
2 eggs
2 1/2 c. sifted all-purpose
    flour

1 t. baking powder
1 t. salt
1 T. lemon zest
    (grated lemon peel)
1 t. lemon flavoring

Blend butter, shortening and sugar. Add eggs and beat. Combine flour, baking powder and salt, adding a small amount at a time to the mixture, blending well. Add zest and flavoring. Chill dough, letting the lemon flavoring set in (overnight is good). Divide dough. On a well floured board, roll out a small quantity at a time to about a 1/4" thickness. Dough not in use should be kept in the refrigerator. Cut into shapes and bake on a lightly greased cookie sheet, for about 10-12 minutes at 375 degrees. Bake until set, but not brown. Sprinkle with colored sugars, before baking, or frost after baking. Dough can be frozen to bake at a later date.

Grandma Smith's Sugar Cookies

Valerie Smith-Kyle

2 c. flour
1/4 t. salt
1/2 t. baking soda
1/4 t. nutmeg

1/2 c. margarine or butter
3/4 c. sugar
1/2 c. sour cream

Combine flour, soda, salt and nutmeg. Cream butter and sugar. Blend in sour cream; and then the dry ingredients. Chill 1 to 2 hours. Divide dough in halves and add food coloring. Roll to 1/2" thick on sugar and floured surface. Cut with favorite cookie cutters; bake on ungreased cookie sheet in a 350 degree oven for 8-10 minutes (on air bake pans bake for 13 minutes). Makes approximately 2 dozen cut-out cookies.

Italian Love Cake

Jackie Hoover

This is delicious...even better a day or two after making, if there is any left over!

1 box fudge marble cake mix
2-15 oz. tubs ricotta cheese
3/4 c. sugar
4 eggs
1 t. vanilla
1 (3 3/4 oz.) pkg. instant pudding (milk chocolate or your choice)
1 c. milk
8 oz. carton whipped topping

Preheat oven to 350 degrees. Grease and flour an 13"x9" pan. Mix cake as directed on package. Pour into pan. Combine ricotta, sugar, eggs and vanilla; mix well. Spoon over unbaked cake. Bake for 1 hour; let cool. Mix pudding with milk, fold in whipped topping; spread over cake. Cover with plastic wrap or foil and store in the refrigerator.

✦Festive Food & Drink✦

Chocolate Torte

Heather Hazen

1 c. toasted chopped pecans
24 vanilla wafers, crushed
1/2 c. butter
1 c. powdered sugar

1 1/2 oz. unsweetened
   chocolate
1 t. vanilla
3 eggs, separated

Mix chopped nuts and crushed vanilla wafers and distribute 1/2 of this mixture in bottom of 8"x8" pan. Cream butter with powdered sugar. Melt chocolate and stir into butter mixture. Add yolks to chocolate mixture one at a time. Beat egg whites until stiff and fold into chocolate mixture. Gently spread over crumb mixture in pan. Distribute remainder of crumbs on top. Refrigerate overnight. Cut in squares and serve with whipped cream.

German Lackerly Cookies

Sara Yosick

Great with hot tea or coffee!

1 lb. honey
2 1/4 c. sugar
1 lb. nuts (about 2 cups)
4 c. flour

1/2 t. nutmeg
1/2 t. ginger
candied fruit (as used
   in fruitcake)

Warm honey, add sugar, stir in nuts, dried ingredients and candied fruit. Roll on floured board and cut with pastry wheel into squares and rectangles. Bake on a lightly greased cookie sheet at 350 degrees for 10 minutes. Frost with glaze made of pulverized sugar (make very fine) and water. Store in covered container. These cookies keep indefinitely and become soft and chewy with age.

New Year Cookies

Jacqueline Lash-Idler

6 oz. semi-sweet chocolate chips
6 oz. butterscotch chips

7 oz. unsalted peanuts
3 1/2 oz. chinese noodles

Melt chips slowly in microwave, stirring frequently. Add peanuts and noodles, mixing thoroughly. Spoon bite-size pieces onto waxed paper and refrigerate. Serve when hard. Store in a cool place.

---

*Bake an apple with lots of cinnamon, brown sugar and raisins...
tastes just like Christmas!*

Holiday Shortbread Drops

Rebecca Chrisman

1 c. butter or margarine,
    softened
1/2 c. granulated sugar
1 egg yolk
2 t. vanilla

1/4 t. salt
2 c. all-purpose flour
1 c. raisins
1 c. chopped walnuts

Cream butter and sugar; blend in egg yolk, vanilla and salt; mix well. Stir in flour. Mix in raisins and walnuts. Drop by small teaspoonsful onto greased baking sheets. Bake at 400 degrees for 10-12 minutes or until delicately browned on the bottom. Makes approximately 4 dozen cookies.

My Three Sons' Christmas Cookies

Judy Borecky

1 c. (2 sticks) margarine or
    butter, softened
    (do not melt in microwave)
2 1/2 c. powdered sugar
2 large eggs

2 1/2 c. flour
1 t. baking soda
1 t. salt
2 t. vanilla extract

Combine all seven ingredients
in a large bowl and beat
until well blended.

Stir in:

1/2 c. vanilla chips
    (white chips)
1 1/2 c. semi-sweet
    chocolate pieces
    or extra large
    chocolate chips
4 chocolate-covered
    toffee candy bars
    (lightly crushed)
1 c. chopped walnuts

Stir with a large spoon and drop on
cookie sheet. Stick or press 3 or 4 salted
macadamia nuts on top or use a couple of
pecan halves instead. Bake in preheated oven at 375
degrees until golden in color, about 12-15 minutes. Makes 35-40 cookies.

175

⋆Festive Food & Drink⋆

Old-Fashioned Iced Sugar Cookies
Lori Goodell

2 c. shortening
2 1/2 c. sugar
1 1/2 t. orange peel
1 1/2 t. vanilla
3 eggs

1/4 c. orange juice
6 c. flour
4 1/2 t. baking powder
3/4 t. salt

Cream together shortening, sugar, orange peel and vanilla. Add eggs to creamed mixture; mix well. Add orange juice and mix. Sift flour, baking powder and salt, add to creamed mixture, and blend. Chill for 2 hours, covered. Once chilled, roll on lightly floured surface 1/8 to 1/4 inch thick. Cut out with favorite cutters. Use floured pancake flap to pick up cut-out cookies and put on ungreased cookie sheet. Bake at 375 degrees for 7-10 minutes. Cool before removing from cookie sheet; ice when cool.

Icing:

1/4 c. butter
4 c. sifted powdered sugar
2 egg whites, unbeaten
1 t. vanilla

1/4 t. cream of tartar
1 to 2 t. light cream or
   canned milk

With a fork, cut margarine into small squares. Add sugar and mix until you get a cornmeal consistency. Add egg whites, vanilla and cream of tartar; beat thoroughly. Stir in cream or milk (add more if too stiff). Divide into separate bowls, add 2 drops of food coloring to each and stir well. Ice cookies and let dry. Once dry, layer cookies in boxes or tins with waxed paper between each layer.

We all love to give gifts, but sometimes as we get older, the task of going out and shopping becomes more difficult. Why not make a box filled with little gifts suitable for all ages and either sex and give it to that someone special? When it comes time to "shop", they simply go to the box and make a selection.

Visions of Sugarplums

Me-Ma's Cookies
Peg Ackerman

When I was little I could not pronounce "my grandmother". I used to call her "Me-Ma". Me-Ma always brought these cookies on Christmas Eve, and somehow they never made it to Christmas dinner. These cookies are what my husband calls "deadly"!

1/2 c. butter or margarine	1 c. packed brown sugar
1 egg	1 t. vanilla
1 3/4 c. flour	3-1 oz. squares unsweetened
1/2 t. baking soda	chocolate
3/4 cup fresh sour cream	1/8 t. salt

Cream butter and sugar until fluffy. Beat in egg and vanilla. Stir in melted chocolate. Sift dry ingredients. Alternating with sour cream, add dry ingredients to the chocolate mixture; mix well. Drop from teaspoon on lightly greased cookie sheet. Bake at 350 degrees 12-14 minutes. Cool on rack.

Frosting:

1/4 lb. margarine, softened	5 T. half-and-half
7 heaping t. unsweetened cocoa	1/8 t. salt
2 c. powdered sugar	1 1/2 t. vanilla

Cream margarine and cocoa. Add 1 cup of powdered sugar, a small amount at a time. Add 3 tablespoons half-and-half and another cup of powdered sugar. Next add the salt and vanilla, and two more tablespoons of half-and-half. If a little stiff, add a little more half-and-half. Decorate with little sprinkles. Makes 3-4 dozen, depending on your teaspoon!

Buttermilk Cookies
Donna Green

1/4 c. margarine	1 c. buttermilk
3/4 c. vegetable shortening	3 1/4 c. flour
1 1/2 c. sugar	1 t. salt
2 eggs	1 t. baking soda
2 t. vanilla	1 t. baking powder

Mix ingredients together. Refrigerate 2-3 hours or overnight. Lightly greased cookie sheets and bake at 375 degrees for 8-10 minutes. Ice with buttercream frosting.

✦Festive Food & Drink✦

14 Layer Chocolate Cake
Phyllis Purvis

The fun of this cake is watching the children count the layers. Sometimes more than 14 and sometimes less are made from the recipe.

1/2 c. vegetable shortening
1 stick margarine
6 eggs
2 c. sugar

1 c. milk
3 c. self-rising flour
2 t. vanilla flavoring

Mix all ingredients as for any layer cake. Batter will be thinner than usual. Put 4 tablespoons of batter into greased and floured cake pans. Bump pans gently with hands to spread batter over the entire pan. Bake at 350 degrees for a very short time (approximately 5 to 7 minutes). Do not cook too long or allow layer to get brown. Partially cool before removing from pans.

Filling:

2 c. sugar
1 1/2 sticks margarine
6 T. cocoa

enough water to make paste
1 1/2 c. evaporated milk

Bring mixture to a rolling boil in a 2-quart sauce pan. Remove from heat and beat with electric mixer for 1/2 minute. Start stacking layers with filling, working quickly. Let filling run down the sides of the cake.

Failproof Peanut Patties
Barbara Loe

1 1/2 c. raw peanuts
1 1/4 c. granulated sugar
1/3 c. light corn syrup
1/2 c. milk

1/2 t. vanilla
1 1/2 t. margarine
red food coloring (optional)

In a large glass microwave-safe batter bowl, mix all ingredients. Microwave on high for 6 minutes. Stir well, microwave on high for 6 more minutes. Stir until thick. Drop onto greased cookie sheet.

Decorate candles with gold and silver foil stars!

178

Snow Pudding

Sharon S. Obenauf

1 pkg. gelatin
1/4 c. cold water
1 c. boiling water
1 1/4 c. sugar
1/4 c. lemon juice

3 egg whites, stiffly beaten
3 egg yolks
1/8 t. salt
2 c. scalded milk
1 t. vanilla

Soak gelatin in cold water, then dissolve in boiling water. Add 1 cup of sugar and lemon juice. Strain all and let cool, stirring occasionally. When thick, beat until frothy. Add whites of 3 stiffly beaten eggs and continue beating until stiff enough to hold shape. Refrigerate until ready to serve.

Custard:

Beat egg yolks slightly, add 1/4 cup of sugar, and salt. Stir constantly while adding scalded milk. Cook in double boiler until thick. When it coats spoon, take off heat and let cool. Add vanilla. Refrigerate.

To serve, put some gelatin-meringue mixture in a bowl, spoon custard over mixture and top with whipped cream and a cherry. You can also fill a pretty pitcher with the custard and pass around the table, for those who would like more than just a spoonful.

Christmas Ice Cream

Michelle Hogan

This is an easy and beautiful way to prepare a simple and light dessert. Put scoops of ice cream in pretty dessert cups. Freeze until ready to serve. Then allow each guest to choose the "Christmas" topping of their choice:

Red - Cinnamon Schnapps
Green - Creme de Menthe
White - Bailey's Irish Creme

You can use other flavors of ice cream or liqueur, if desired.

✦Festive Food & Drink✦

Miniature Tea Pastries

Carolyn Ritz Lemon

Crust:

1 c. butter or margarine
2 c. all-purpose flour
6 oz. cream cheese

2 t. sugar
1 c. pecans, chopped fine
2 t. vanilla

All ingredients must be at room temperature. Mix like a pie crust. Chill 1 hour. Pinch 48 balls and mold into small muffin tin.

Filling:

2 eggs, beaten
1 1/2 c. light brown sugar
2 T. butter, softened

In a medium bowl mix ingredients together. Pour small amounts into small, pastry lined muffin tin. Bake for 25 minutes at 325 degrees or until brown.

Gingerbread Cookies

Joyce Newburn

1 c. brown sugar
1 c. light molasses
1 c. shortening (not oil), melted
1 egg, beaten
1 t. ginger

1 t. cinnamon
1/2 c. hot water
1 T. baking soda
pinch of salt
5 c. flour

Mix sugar, molasses, melted shortening, beaten egg, ginger, salt, cinnamon, 1/2 cup hot water and baking soda; mix well. Add flour to make a soft dough. Chill for 1 to 2 hours. Roll out and cut with gingerbread boy (or girl!) cookie cutter (from Gooseberry Patch, of course). Sprinkle on granulated sugar before baking. Bake in 350 degree oven for 10 to 12 minutes. Yield: 3 to 4 dozen cookies, really depends on size of cutter and how thick you make the cookies (the thicker cookie is softer).

Holiday Squares

Emily R. McLaughlin

1 1/2 c. sugar
1 c. butter (not margarine),
    softened
4 eggs

2 c. flour
2 t. almond extract
1 can cherry pie filling

Gradually add sugar to softened butter, add eggs one at a time. Add other ingredients, except pie filling. Spread in a well-greased jelly roll pan (or cookie sheet 10"x15"x1" or 17"x11"x1"). Mark off 20-24 squares. Spoon filling into each square. Bake at 350 degrees for 25-30 minutes. When cooled, sprinkle with powdered sugar. For variation, blueberries can be used.

Spicy Molasses Drop Cookies

Dorothy Hender

1/2 c. margarine
1 c. sugar
1/2 c. molasses
1 t. baking soda, dissolved in
    1/2 c. of warm water
1 t. ground cloves
1 t. cinnamon
3 c. flour
1 c. raisins (optional)

Cream margarine and sugar. Add the molasses and baking soda, mixing well. Sift together the cloves, cinnamon and flour; add to molasses mixture gradually until well blended. Drop batter by rounded teaspoonsful onto a greased cookie sheet. Do not place too close together, as the batter spreads a little. Sprinkle some sugar on top of each cookie and bake at 350 degrees for 12-16 minutes depending on your oven. Cookies are done when slightly firm to the touch. Makes about 3 dozen cookies.

✦Festive Food & Drink✦

Easy Plum Pudding
Diane Dollak

1/3 c. butter or margarine
2/3 c. brown sugar
2 eggs
1 c. biscuit baking mix
2 t. grated orange rind
3/4 t. cinnamon
3/4 t. nutmeg

1/2 c. rum or brandy (or apple cider)
1/2 c. pitted dried prunes, cut
1 c. fine soft bread crumbs
3/4 c. chopped walnuts
1 c. applesauce
1/4 t. cloves
1 c. raisins

Mix all ingredients and pour into a well greased 1 1/2-quart mold. Cover tightly with aluminum foil and place on a rack in a large kettle. Add hot water to 1/3 the depth of the mold. Cover the kettle and steam the pudding for 2 1/2 hours, adding water as necessary. Serve with a hard sauce, or a lemon sauce. Pudding can be made well in advance and frozen (wrapped in foil). Reheat in the oven or by steaming.

Hard Sauce:

2/3 c. butter
2 1/2 c. powdered sugar
enough rum to make a
    thick sauce

Combine ingredients.

Lemon Sauce:

1/2 c. sugar
1 T. cornstarch
1 c. water
1 T. butter
1 T. lemon juice
1 T. grated lemon rind

Combine sugar, cornstarch and cold water. Bring to a boil, stirring constantly and boil for 1 minute. Remove from heat and stir in remaining ingredients.

Orange Spice Cake

Leona Keeley

1/2 c. vegetable shortening
1 c. sugar
2 large eggs
2 c. flour
1/2 t. salt
1 t. baking soda
1 t. cinnamon

1/2 t. cloves
1/2 t. allspice
2/3 c. sour milk (1 T. white
    vinegar in 2/3 c. milk)
1/3 c. orange juice
1/2 c. walnuts and raisins

Cream shortening, add sugar and eggs. Add dry ingredients. Stir in sour milk, alternating with orange juice; beat well, add raisins and nuts. Pour into a tube pan, bake at 350 degrees for 45 minutes. Yields: 10-12 servings.

Aunt Libby's Rum Cake

Juanita Williams

1 c. black walnuts
1 pkg. butter recipe golden
    cake mix
1 (3 3/4 oz.) pkg. instant
    vanilla pudding

1/2 c. light rum
1/2 c. cooking oil
4 eggs
1/2 c. water

Grease and flour bundt pan. Spread nuts onto bottom of pan. Place cake mix, pudding and all other ingredients in a pan and mix for 2 minutes. Bake 40-50 minutes at 350 degrees. Take cake from oven and let cool for 20 minutes before you remove to serving platter.

Top with Hot Rum Glaze:

1 c. sugar
1/4 c. rum

1 stick butter
1/4 c. water

Put in saucepan and boil 2 or 3 minutes and pour over the cake.

Include kids in your holiday party...have it in the afternoon and serve cookies and Christmas punch.

Festive Food & Drink

Old-Fashioned Fruitcake

Cheryl Neff

2 c. pecans, do not chop
3/4 lb. candied pineapple
3/4 lb. whole candied cherries
1 1/2 lbs. ready mix candied fruit
1 bottle (1 oz.) brandy flavoring
1 lb. seedless raisins
1 t. nutmeg

1 1/2 t. cinnamon
6 eggs
2 1/2 c. white sugar
1/2 lb. butter
4 c. flour
1 t. salt

Line baking pan (angel food) with foil. Have nuts and fruit ready. Mix butter, sugar, eggs and flavoring in a large bowl with electric mixer. Sift together remaining ingredients and mix thoroughly with butter and egg mixture. Work the fruits and nuts into batter with hands. Fill pan 2/3 full with batter. Bake at 275 degrees for 3 hours. One-half hour before cake is done, brush top with light corn syrup. Decorate with pecan halves and finish baking. Cool. Place in an airtight container, wrapped in a wine soaked cloth. Store in a cool place for several weeks, this blends and mellows the cake.

Lemon Coconut Squares

Marlene Wetzel-Dellagatta

1 c. all-purpose flour
1/2 c. margarine or butter,
    softened
1/4 c. powdered sugar
1 c. granulated sugar
2 eggs

2 t. grated lemon peel
2 T. lemon juice
1/2 t. baking powder
1/4 t. salt
1/2 c. flaked coconut

Preheat oven to 350 degrees. Mix flour, margarine, and powdered sugar. Press in ungreased 8"x8"x2" baking pan, building up 1/2" edges. Bake 20 minutes. Beat remaining ingredients until light and fluffy (about 3 minutes), pour over baked layer. Bake until no indentation remains when touched in center (about 25 minutes). Cool, cut into 1" squares. Makes about 4 dozen.

"A friend is a present you give yourself."

Poinsettia Desserts

Ginger Fulton

small terra cotta flower pots
ice cream (lime sherbert or
    pistachio is Christmasy)

clear plastic straws
paper or styrofoam cups
chocolate sandwich cookies

You will need several small terra cotta flower pots (one for each Poinsettia
Dessert you are making). Line one of them with a paper or styrofoam cup
(you may need to trim the top so that it isn't taller than the flower pot).
Take the cup back out of the flower pot and set the pot aside. Cut as many
cups as you will need to the same size. Soften ice cream. Fill the cups 3/4"
full of softened ice cream. Then insert a clear plastic straw upright in the
middle of each cup. Using a blender or a rolling pin over a plastic bag,
crunch up the chocolate sandwich cookies; sprinkle crunched up cookies
over the ice cream layer. This will look like potting soil (nutrition-conscious
people can substitute carob cookies). Place cups in the freezer until just
before serving. Now you can decorate your terra cotta flower pots using foil
paper in red or green and a pretty Christmas bow for each. Purchase either
real or artificial poinsettias to have ready for each dessert. Just before serving remove cups from freezer, place in decorated flower pots and place
poinsettia blooms in the clear plastic straw. Bring your Poinsettia Desserts
to your guests on a tray and watch the surprised expressions on their faces.

Coconut Macaroons

Kara Kimerline

2/3 c. (1/2 of 15 oz. can)
    sweetened condensed milk
3 c. shredded coconut

1 t. vanilla extract
3/4 t. almond extract

Mix together condensed milk, coconut, and flavorings. Drop by teaspoonsful, about 1" apart, on a well greased cookie sheet. Bake at 350 degrees for
8-10 minutes, or until delicately browned around the edges. Remove from
baking sheet immediately. Makes about 30 cookies.

⋆Festive Food & Drink⋆

Christmas Cheesecake

Patricia Kinghorn

This recipe has the advantage of making delicious cheesecake without the bother of a springform pan.

Crust:

1/2 c. white flour
1/3 c. softened butter
1/2 c. brown sugar

Combine flour, butter and sugar; pat in an ungreased 8" square pan (or use a round pan). Bake at 350 degrees for 8-10 minutes. Remove from oven.

Filling:

2- 8 oz. pkgs. cream
    cheese, softened
1/2 c. sugar
2 large eggs
4 T. milk or cream
2 T. lemon juice
1 t. vanilla

Using an electric mixer, combine ingredients until smooth. Spread over partially baked crust. Bake 30-35 minutes more at 350 degrees.

Hello Dollies

Marlene Wetzel-Dellagatta

1 stick margarine
1 c. graham cracker crumbs
1 c. flaked coconut
6 oz. pkg. semi-sweet
    chocolate chips

1 c. chopped walnuts
14 oz. can sweetened
    condensed milk

Preheat oven to 350 degrees. Melt margarine in an 8"x8"x2" pan. Put in layers: graham cracker crumbs, coconut, nuts and chocolate chips. Pour sweetened condensed milk evenly over all. Bake 25-30 minutes. Makes approximately 4 dozen.

> *"I'm dreaming of a white Christmas."*
> *Irving Berlin*

Visions of Sugarplums

Get Your Moose Chocolate Style
A real chocolate mousse pie, that is!

Peg Huffman
Gooseberry Patch Artisan

This is an original recipe developed and written by my dad. He gave it to me years ago and I have handed it down to my daughter. He definitely has his own style.

Here's the stuff you're going to need:
2-qt. sized mixing bowl
wooden spoon, about 10" long
one measuring teaspoon
1/2 c. measuring cup
1/3 measuring cup
8 oz. container frozen
   whipped topping
3 oz. pkg. cream cheese
1 t. vanilla
1/3 c. cocoa
1/3 c. milk
1/2 c. sugar
one ready pie crust (any flavor, but I like graham cracker best!)

Before gettin' started on this masterpiece, get the cream cheese out of the fridge and the frozen whipped topping out of the freezer. Let these come up to room temperature for an hour or two. While they're warmin' up, you can put all the other stuff out on your work bench...won't hurt anything! After an hour or two, wait for the warmin' up of the cream cheese and whipped topping and get started! Take the plastic cover off your ready pie crust and wash this cover, so when you cover your finished product with it, the clean side will be towards the mousse pie. Keep the pie crust in its aluminum container nearby, ready to receive the filling. Get a mixing bowl, oh, about the size that will hold 2 quarts of water. I use a wooden spoon to do the mixing that follows, but you could use an electric mixer (remember, it's easier to lick the spoon than those gadgets on the electric mixer!) Dump in the cream cheese, sugar, vanilla, cocoa and then the milk and start mixin' it. Better do it so that the milk is last 'cause it'll all mix easier. Do it near your sink in case you splatter, like I do. I admit that it takes longer to use the wooden spoon, but I'm not in a hurry! After it looks pretty well mixed, start adding the whipped topping a few spoonsful at a time and keep mixin'. Finally get all the whipped topping mixed in. When you think you've done your best mixing job, carefully dump it into the ready pie crust. Now put the clean plastic cover on this beauty and put it in your freezer or fridge. Personally, I like it best when frozen like ice cream. OK, now the fun starts...thoroughly lick the spoon and mixin' bowl! Oh yes, be sure to share the pie.

✦Festive Food & Drink✦

Snow Ice Cream
Juanita Williams

*with love & sweet memories
from Grandma & Grandpa*

1 c. heavy cream
sugar

vanilla extract
1 qt. (4 c.) perfectly clean snow

One of the greatest treats in life is to sit by a warm fire and eat snow ice cream. All you need to remember is to gather good clean snow. Whip up heavy cream, fold in sugar and vanilla extract, to taste. Take a large bowl outside and scoop up snow, while the snow is still frozen. Fold snow into the cream mixture and adjust the sugar and vanilla, to taste. Eat immediately or pack the bowl outside your door in a snowbank (well covered to protect the ice cream from wild or domestic animals), and let it chill until the ice cream has hardened. Makes about 6 servings.

Frosty Strawberry Squares
Norma Anderson

1 c. flour
1/2 c. chopped walnuts

1/2 c. brown sugar
1/2 c. margarine

Mix all together and spread evenly in shallow baking pan. Bake in 350 degree oven for 20 minutes, stirring occasionally. After it cools, sprinkle 2/3 of the crumbs in a 13"x9"x2" baking dish.

Strawberry Mixture:

2 egg whites
1 c. sugar
1 tub frozen whipped
    topping, thawed

2 T. lemon juice
10 oz. pkg. frozen strawberries
    (partially thawed)

Beat egg whites until stiff. Add other ingredients and beat at high speed with electric mixer about 10 minutes. Fold in whipped topping. Spoon over crumbs and sprinkle remaining crumbs on top. Freeze overnight; cut into squares. May be garnished with whole strawberries.

Go outside, play in the snow and come in by the fire for a cup of hot mulled cider or cocoa. Add whipped cream, a candy cane or cinnamon stick for extra flavor and a little fun!

Frozen Peanut Butter Pie

Barb Agne
Gooseberry Patch

8 oz. pkg. cream cheese, softened
1 c. powdered sugar
1/3 c. creamy peanut butter (more if desired)
1/2 c. milk
9 oz. container frozen whipped topping
9" pie crust (graham cracker or chocolate)

Whip cream cheese until fluffy. Beat in powdered
sugar and peanut butter. Gradually add milk,
blending well. Fold in whipped topping. Put in
pie crust; freeze until firm.

Sour Cream Peach Pie

Hazel Hayden
Gooseberry Patch Artisan

2 c. peaches, canned or fresh
3/4 c. sugar
2 T. flour
1 c. sour cream
1 egg, beaten
1/4 t. vanilla

Combine all ingredients. Spoon
into a 9" pie shell. Bake at 350
degrees for 35 minutes. Sprinkle
on topping. Bake 10 minutes
more and cool.

Topping:

1/4 c. butter
1/3 c. flour
1/3 c. brown sugar
1/4 t. nutmeg
1/4 t. cinnamon
1/4 t. cloves

Combine all ingredients.

Festive Food & Drink

Egg Nog Pie

Jeannine English

9" unbaked pie shell
3 eggs
1 can sweetened condensed milk
1 1/4 c. very hottest tap water

1 t. vanilla
1/4 t. salt
1/8 t. nutmeg

Preheat oven to 425 degrees. Bake pie shell for 8 minutes. Remove from oven. In a bowl, beat eggs, condensed milk, water, vanilla, salt and nutmeg. Pour into pie shell. Bake at 425 degrees for 10 minutes; reduce heat to 350 degrees and continue baking for 25 additional minutes, or until knife inserted in center of pie comes out clean.

Paper Bag Apple Pie

Lisa Glenn

4-5 apples (2 1/2 lbs.), sliced
   and peeled
1/2 c. sugar
2 T. flour

1 t. nutmeg
1 t. cinnamon
2 T. lemon juice
unbaked pie shell

Place apples in a large bowl. Combine sugar, flour, nutmeg and cinnamon and sprinkle over apples. Toss to coat well. Put into pie shell. Drizzle with lemon juice. Sprinkle topping over apples. Slide pie into a large brown paper grocery bag. Fold end and staple shut. Place on cookie sheet. Bake at 400 degrees for 1 hour. Split bag open; remove to cool. Very good and the mess is inside the bag. Makes 1 pie.

Topping:

1/2 c. sugar
1/2 c. flour
1/2 c. butter

Combine sugar and flour. Cut in butter and sprinkle evenly over apples.

French Apple Creme Pie

Carolyn Ritz Lemon

Start with a two crust unbaked pie shell, roll bottom half and put into pie tin. Roll top half and cut a two inch opening in the center. You can use a large, favorite holiday cookie cutter to make this opening, then put aside.

Apple Filling:

3/4 c. sugar	1 T. grated lemon rind
2 T. flour	5 c. Granny Smith apples
1/2 t. cinnamon	2 T. butter
1/2 t. nutmeg	

Combine sugar, flour, cinnamon, nutmeg and lemon rind in a large bowl. Add apples and stir to coat. Turn into pie shell and dot with butter. Top with pie crust that has a two inch opening cut into the center. Bake for 10 minutes at 425 degrees and then 30-35 minutes at 375 degrees. While your pie is baking, cook the creme sauce.

Creme Sauce:

2 eggs, beaten	3 oz. cream cheese,
1/2 c. sugar	cut into pieces
1 T. lemon juice	1/2 c. sour cream

In a saucepan combine eggs, sugar, and lemon juice. Cook over medium heat, stirring constantly until thick. Add cream cheese and sour cream. After your pie is baked, spoon through opening at top of crust. Chill before serving.

Chewy Pecan Pie

Barbara Loe

9" pastry pie shell	1/4 c. milk
1 c. brown sugar	2 c. broken pecans
1/3 c. margarine	1/2 t. vanilla
1/3 c. light corn syrup	

In a heavy saucepan, stir together brown sugar, margarine, corn syrup and milk. Bring to a boil over medium heat and stir often. Do not stir while it boils for 2 minutes. Remove from heat. Stir in pecans and vanilla. Pour into prepared pie shell. Bake at 350 degrees for 15-20 minutes or until bubbly and the crust is done. Cool. You can pre-bake pie shell partially, but I don't.

·Festive Food & Drink·

Butterscotch Pie

Barbara Loe

1 c. brown sugar
2 T. water
1/4 t. salt
2 c. cold milk, divided
1/4 c. cornstarch

2 egg yolks, beaten
2 T. margarine
1/2 t. vanilla
1 baked 9" pastry shell

Cook brown sugar, water and salt over very low heat in a medium saucepan, until thick and syrupy. Stir together 1/4 cup milk and the cornstarch to form a smooth paste. Stir in remaining 1 3/4 cups milk. Add to brown sugar mixture and continue cooking, stirring constantly, until mixture thickens. Cook and stir for an additional 15 minutes. Stir a small amount of hot mixture into beaten egg yolks, and return to heat for 3 minutes. Remove from heat and stir in margarine and vanilla. Cool to lukewarm. Turn into pie shell. Top with meringue.

Meringue:

2 egg whites   4 T. brown sugar   1/2 t. vanilla

Beat egg whites until stiff peaks form. Gradually beat in brown sugar. Stir in vanilla. Pile onto pie filling in shell, being careful to seal edges to pie crust. Bake at 325 degrees for 15 minutes or until browned.

Betsye's Lemon Pie

Debra Kreul

2 eggs, separated
1 can sweetened
    condensed milk
1/2 c. lemon juice
1 t. lemon peel, grated

1 graham cracker crust
nutmeg
1/4 t. cream of tartar
1/4 c. sugar

Preheat oven to 350 degrees. Beat egg yolks in a medium size mixing bowl. Add milk, lemon juice, and lemon peel and mix well. Pour into graham cracker crust and sprinkle with nutmeg. Beat egg whites and cream of tartar together; gradually add sugar until stiff. Pour into pie crust. Bake for 15 minutes, or until pie turns brown. Yields: 1 pie.

Host a holiday dessert party. Invite your friends for 8:00 and serve several different desserts with coffee, brandy and dessert wines. Fruit and cheese are nice accompaniments.

Gifts From The Kitchen

✦Festive Food & Drink✦

Cocktail Walnuts
Judy Carter

3 T. salad oil
8 oz. walnuts
2 t. celery salt

1/4 t. garlic powder
1/4 t. cayenne pepper

In a skillet, heat the salad oil, stir in the walnuts and saute. Stir constantly, until crisp. Remove nuts with a slotted spoon. Mix together salt, garlic powder and pepper. Toss nuts in this mixture.

Chocolate Topped Toffee
Cathy Pratt

1/2 c. butter
1/2 t. salt
1 c. sugar

1/4 c. water
12 oz. chocolate chips
chopped pecans or almonds

Combine butter, salt, sugar and water in a 2-quart pan. Cook over medium heat, stirring constantly, until mixture boils. Cook without stirring until mixture reaches 285 degrees Fahrenheit (light crack stage). Pour onto greased cookie sheet and cool until set. Melt chocolate chips and spread half over toffee. Sprinkle with 1/2 of chopped nuts. Chill until set and then loosen toffee with knife and flip over. Spread the rest of the chocolate on this side and sprinkle the rest of the nuts over top. Chill until set. Break into bite-size pieces and store in an airtight container. Easy and delicious.

Peanut Butter Penuche
Betty Monfort

3/4 c. milk
1 lb. light brown sugar
2 c. white sugar

12 oz. crunchy peanut butter
3 T. marshmallow fluff
2 t. vanilla

Combine the milk and sugars; boil for 3 minutes. Add the peanut butter. Add the fluff and vanilla; beat for a short time. Pour into 9"x9" pan.

Host a Christmas Workshop. Turn your home in to a present-making factory by setting up card tables with rubber stamps, inks, colored pencils, sparkles, scraps of fabrics, ribbon and paints. Have a fun time making cards, gift wrap and ornaments.

Bavarian Mint Coffee Mix

Cheryl Ewer

1/3 c. nondairy creamer
1/3 c. sugar
1/3 c. instant coffee

2 T. cocoa
5 hard peppermint candies,
crushed

Combine all together. Store in airtight container. Use 2 to 2 1/2 teaspoons per cup of boiling water. Relax and enjoy!

Vanilla Coffee

Judy Borecky

1 1/2 c. dry coffee creamer
1 c. dry hot chocolate mix
1/2 t. nutmeg
1 t. cinnamon

1 1/2 c. sugar
1/2 c. instant coffee crystals
2 T. vanilla powder

Mix all ingredients together and place in cellophane bags. When ready to use, put 2 or 4 tablespoons in a mug of boiling water and enjoy. If you wish to use sugar substitute instead of sugar, omit sugar from ingredients and add sugar substitute (to taste) in mug.

Susan's Pumpkin Butter

Elenna Firme
Gooseberry Patch Artisan

This recipe is very much like apple butter and has a better flavor if made with fresh pumpkin. We like it better than apple butter. Serve with warm, fresh bread or biscuits.

3 1/2 c. cooked or canned pumpkin
4 1/2 c. sugar
1 T. pumpkin pie spice
1 box clear jelling agent

Measure pumpkin into a large sauce pan. Measure sugar and set aside. Add spice and jelling agent to pumpkin and mix well. Place over high heat, stir until mixture comes to a boil (it will never probably come to a rolling boil...just a plop plop). Immediately add the sugar and stir in well. Bring to a rolling boil and boil hard for 1 minute, stirring constantly. Remove from heat and ladle into jars. Cover with paraffin. Makes about 5 1/2 cups.

✦Festive Food ⅋ Drink✦

Hot Pepper Jelly

Terrie Rasmussen

This looks "holiday special" and it tastes so good. Pack it with a wooden serving spoon. It's great with cream cheese and unsalted crackers.

1 1/2 c. chopped green
   pepper, seeded
4 oz. can chili peppers,
   drained
1 1/2 c. cider vinegar
6 1/2 c. sugar
1/8 t. green food
   coloring
2 3-oz. pouches
   liquid fruit
   pectin

Put peppers and chilies in blender or food processor. Cover and process until pureed. In a stainless or enameled saucepan heat sugar and vinegar until the sugar dissolves. Add pepper puree and bring to a boil over high heat. Reduce heat to moderately low and let simmer for 5 minutes. Stir in food coloring, skim off and discard foam. Remove from heat and stir in pectin. Pour into 8 1/2-pint sterilized jars, filling each to within 1/8" of the top. Seal jars with lids and screw bands or rubber rings and clamp tops. Cool upright on wire racks. Makes about 8 1/2-pint jars.

Christmas Brew
Recipe for Holiday Fragrance

Georgene Kornreich
Gooseberry Patch Artisan

I've come to be known as the dessert queen of the east coast. So my friends and family expect something from my kitchen along with a package of my "Christmas Brew" that fills their houses with a scent that says, "Welcome friends."

1 T. pickle spice
 (remove pepper)
2 t. lemon and orange peel
a couple of cinnamon sticks
pinch of cinnamon oil

1 T. whole cloves
1 T. ginger
1 bay leaf
1 T. allspice
4 c. boiling water

Put ingredients in a crockpot. Your house will smell just wonderful. If the scent starts to leave, add just a bit more cinnamon oil. This mixture will last for days. As the water evaporates, add more. May also be kept in a jar in the refrigerator when not in use.

Orange-Cranberry Marmalade

Terrie Rasmussen

In a 2-qt. saucepan, over high heat, place 2 cups of fresh cranberries, 2/3 cup orange juice, 2 teaspoons grated orange peel, and 1/2 cup sugar, bringing to a boil. Reduce heat to low, cover and simmer until cranberries pop and mixture thickens slightly, (about 20 minutes) stirring occasionally. Store in refrigerator in heat-proof jar. Makes 1 1/2 cups. Place in a cute antique jar tied with a ribbon.

Pasta Oil

Joanne Jacobellis

Tasty in pasta salads.

3 sprigs sage
2 cloves garlic
1 small bunch parsley
1 small hot red pepper

5 oz. parmesan cheese
 cut in small chunks
1 qt. extra-virgin olive oil

Makes 1 quart.

✦Festive Food & Drink✦

Swedish Almond Braid

Marilyn Hintz

3 pkgs. active dry yeast
1/2 c. very warm water
3/4 c. milk
1 egg

1/3 c. sugar
1 t. salt
4 c. sifted regular flour
3/4 lb. (3 sticks) very cold butter

Preheat oven to 450 degrees. Sprinkle or crumble yeast into very warm water in a large bowl. Stir until dissolved. Add milk, egg, salt and sugar. Stir in 3 1/4 cups of the flour to make a soft dough. Beat vigorously for 2 minutes; roll out on floured board. Cut butter in slices and lay on 2/3 of dough; fold over and roll. Repeat folding and rolling 3 more times. Cut dough into 4 equal portions. Roll each portion into 9"x12" rectangle. Slice each rectangle lengthwise into three 12" strips. Spread rounded teaspoon of almond paste on each strip. Fold each strip over almond paste and seal. Braid the 3 strips together (from each of the 4 rectangles). Place 2 completed braids on a large cookie sheet, spaced equally apart. Allow to rise until doubled. Brush with egg yolk. Sprinkle with sugar and slice almonds. Lower oven temperature to 375 degrees and bake braids for 25 minutes. Makes four 12"x4" braids.

Almond Paste:

**1 egg white
1/2 c. almond
     paste
1/2 c. sugar**

Slightly beat egg white in a small bowl. Stir in paste and sugar. Mix slightly with a fork or until well blended. Yield: Enough to fill 2 braids.

Poppy Seed Bread

Nancy McGrew

3 c. flour
2 1/4 c. sugar
1 1/8 c. vegetable oil
1 1/2 c. milk
3 eggs
1 T. poppy seed

1 t. salt
1 t. baking powder
1 1/2 t. vanilla flavoring
1 1/2 t. almond flavoring
1 1/2 t. butter flavoring

Preheat oven to 375 degrees. Grease and flour 2 loaf pans or 3 pans that measure 7 1/2"x3 1/2"x2". Mix all ingredients together thoroughly. Pour into pans and bake 1 hour and 10 to 15 minutes at 375 degrees.

Glaze (optional):

1 1/2 t. butter flavoring
1/4 c. orange juice
3/4 c. sugar
1 1/2 t. almond flavoring

Mulling Spice Bags

Jacqueline Lash-Idler

4 cinnamon sticks
8 whole allspice
8 whole cloves
4 T. grated orange peel
cheesecloth & butcher's twine

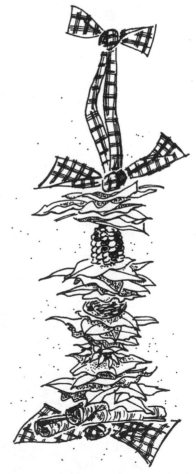

Cut cheesecloth in double thickness into 4"x6" squares. Place onto each square 1 cinnamon stick, 2 cloves, 2 allspice and 1 tablespoon orange peel. Then bundle up with twine. Buy 1 gallon of cider and place in a basket along with the mulling spice. Top with a festive bow.

⋆Festive Food & Drink⋆

Holiday Cocoa
Jacqueline Lash-Idler

A pair of mugs and a tin of holiday cookies would go nicely with this gift.

6 c. unsweetened cocoa
2 c. malted milk powder
7 c. granulated sugar

2 T. cinnamon
1 vanilla bean, split in half

Blend all ingredients and let sit for 3 days. Spoon 3 cups into 5 gift jars. Include these instructions with your gift: Mix 1/4 cup of mix into an 8-10 oz. mug of hot milk.

Thyme, Lemon Peel & Black Pepper Vinegar
Jacqueline Lash-Idler

For an extra special touch, I tie ribbons or raffia around the necks of my vinegars and label them.

1 large sprig fresh thyme
1 long spiral lemon peel

2 heaping T. black peppercorns
2 c. white wine vinegar

Herbal vinegars are visually appealing as well as tasty in salads and as marinades in various dishes. White wine vinegar is delicate in taste and I consider it to be the best in the making of vinegars. Place herbs in 1 pint, sterilized jars (you can use soda bottles with plastic re-sealable tops or wine bottles with new, cork tops). Boil bottles in water to sterilize. Add vinegar and seal tightly. Place in light filled window for one month, giving bottles a gentle shake every so often.

Citrus or Orange Butter

Juanita Rieser

A very nice spread for toast at Christmas brunch!

1 lb. sweet butter,
   room temperature
4 c. powdered sugar

1/2 c. orange juice
1/2 c. orange rind, fresh
4 t. lemon juice

Mix butter and sugar until blended very smooth and soft. Slowly add the orange juice, orange rind, and lemon juice. You may substitute stick margarine for butter.

◆Festive Food & Drink◆

Gift of the Magi Bread
Pat Milliman

1/2 c. butter or margarine
1 c. granulated sugar
2 eggs
1 t. vanilla
2 c. flour
1 t. baking soda
pinch of salt (I omit)
1 c. mashed banana

1 can mandarin orange segments,
   drained
6 oz. chocolate chips
1 c. shredded coconut
1/2 c. sliced almonds
   (can use walnuts or pecans)
1/2 c. chopped
   maraschino cherries

Preheat oven to 350 degrees. Cream butter or margarine with sugar. Add eggs and vanilla; beat until fluffy. Sift flour with soda and salt. Add alternately to the creamed mixture, with bananas. Stir in orange segments, nuts, cherries, chocolate chips and coconut. Pour into 2 greased loaf pans. Bake at 350 degrees for 1 to 1 1/4 hours. Makes 2 loaves.

Puppy Chow Snack
for people!
Barb Agne
Gooseberry Patch

8 oz. bite-size crispy
   rice cereal squares
1 stick margarine

6 oz. chocolate chips
1/2 c. peanut butter
2 c. confectioner's sugar

Put cereal squares in a large bowl. Melt margarine, chips, and peanut butter together; pour over cereal squares and mix well. Put sugar into a paper bag, pour cereal mixture in bag and shake. Put finished snack into a bowl.

Divinity
Karen Moran

2 1/2 c. sugar
1/2 c. light corn syrup
1/2 c. water

2 egg whites, stiffly beaten
1 t. vanilla
1 c. chopped nuts

Cook sugar, syrup and water until it spins a thread. Remove from heat; add egg whites, vanilla and chopped nuts. Beat until it stiffens. Drop by teaspoonful on greased paper or pour in greased pan. To stiffen quicker, set pot in cool water.

Turn out all the lights and tell stories by the fire.

Marshmallow Cut-Outs

Sue Welch

4 envelopes unflavored gelatin
1 1/2 c. water
3 c. sugar
1 1/4 c. light corn syrup

1/4 t. salt
2 t. vanilla
1 1/2 c. confectioner's sugar

Spray a 13"x9" baking dish with non-stick spray, line dish with waxed paper and spray waxed paper, or you may use foil. Soften gelatin in 3/4 c. water. Place the remaining water, sugar, corn syrup, salt, and vanilla into a heavy saucepan, bring to a boil and cook over high heat until the syrup reaches 234-240 degrees Fahrenheit on a candy thermometer. Beat the hot mixture slowly into the softened gelatin until very stiff (about 10 minutes). Pour mixture into prepared dish and smooth with a spatula. Set aside, uncovered or overnight. At room temperature, using a sifter, sprinkle confectioner's sugar onto a cutting board. Turn the mixture onto the sugar. Then use cookie cutters (I use my star and heart cookie cutters from Gooseberry Patch, of course) to cut into shapes. Dip cut edges of marshmallows into sugar to prevent sticking. These marshmallows are adorable floating in hot chocolate. Yield: About 25 marshmallows, depending on the size of your cookie cutters.

Yummy Caramel Corn

Donna Green

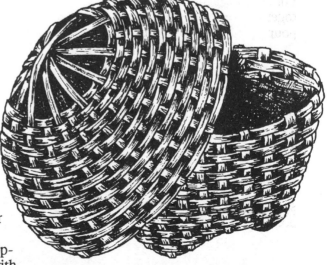

2 c. dark brown sugar
2 sticks margarine
1/4 t. salt
6 T. white corn syrup
1/4 t. baking soda
1/2 t. vanilla
8 oz. no hull popcorn, popped

Melt margarine, add all other ingredients except popcorn; bring to a full boil. Divide popcorn into two bowls, cover with mixture and mix well. Place on two greased jelly roll pans and bake at 225 degrees for 1 hour. Cool and store in an airtight container.

Festive Food & Drink

Becky's Caramels
Rebecca Suiter

A tradition in my family for the last 25 years.

3 c. white corn syrup
4 c. sugar
1 lb. butter (not margarine)
2 c. cream

1 t. salt
1 qt. chopped pecans
2 t. vanilla

In a large 6-quart dutch oven mix the syrup, sugar and butter, and one cup of the cream. Cook over medium to medium high heat for 15 minutes, then add the other cup of cream and the salt. Cook until 245 degrees, or hard ball stage is reached. Before removing from heat, add the pecans and vanilla. Pour into 2 buttered jelly roll pans. When cool, cut into squares. Wrap in waxed paper. Makes a very large amount, plenty to share and tuck into gift baskets.

White Chocolate Fudge
Glenna Ryder

2 c. white sugar
3/4 c. sour cream
1/2 c. unsalted butter
14 oz. white chocolate

7 oz. jar marshmallow cream
1 to 1 1/2 c. walnuts,
    coarsely broken

Combine sugar, sour cream and butter in pan with heavy bottom. Bring mixture to a rolling boil, stirring constantly. Boil for 7 minutes over medium heat, stirring continuously. Remove pan from heat and stir in white chocolate until completely melted. Add marshmallow cream and walnuts. Beat by hand until completely blended. Spread into a greased 9"x9" square pan. Cool at room temperature. Makes approximately 2 1/2 lbs.

Sweet and Crunchy Walnuts
Betty Monfort

1 to 1 1/2 lbs. walnuts
2 large egg whites

1 c. packed brown sugar
1/4 c. butter or margarine, melted

Beat (room temperature) egg whites until stiff. Gradually add melted margarine or butter and brown sugar. Beat until well blended. Stir in walnuts and mix until all are coated with egg white mixture. Turn out onto large jelly roll pan which has been sprayed with a non-stick vegetable spray. Bake in 275 degree oven for 1 hour, stirring every 15 minutes. Cool and store in plastic bag or covered container.

Heavenly Fudge

Sharon Weyand

2 1/4 c. sugar
3/4 c. evaporated milk
2- 6 oz. pkgs. semi-sweet
    chocolate chips

1/3 c. white corn syrup
2 T. butter
1 t. vanilla
1 c. chopped nuts

Combine milk and sugar in heavy saucepan. Cook over medium heat, stirring constantly, until mixture boils. Turn heat to low and continue cooking for 10 minutes, stirring constantly to prevent scorching. Remove from heat and immediately add chocolate chips, syrup, butter and vanilla. Stir until chips melt and fudge is creamy. Add nuts. Pour into buttered 8"x8"x2" pan. Chill for 1/2 hour and cut into squares.

Snowflake Pecans

Linda Zell

1 stick margarine
3 egg whites
1 c. sugar
3 c. whole pecan halves

Preheat oven to 325 degrees. On a jelly roll pan (10"x15"x1") cut up the margarine into small pieces, and put into oven to melt. Meanwhile, beat the 3 egg whites with an electric mixer, gradually adding the sugar until a stiff meringue forms. Fold in the pecans. Very carefully, add the nut mixture to the melted margarine; combine well. Bake for 30 minutes, stirring every 10 minutes. Cool nuts on waxed paper, separating them. Store in a tightly covered container.

"Bah," said Scrooge. "Humbug!"
Charles Dickens

·Festive Food & Drink·

Cashew Brittle
Margaret Riley

1 c. cashews
1/2 c. butter or stick margarine

1/2 c. sugar
1 T. light corn syrup

Combine everything in medium saucepan. Bring to a boil over medium heat. Continue to boil; stirring constantly 5 to 6 minutes, or until golden brown. Pour quickly and spread in a 8" or 9" foil-lined and buttered pan. Cool 15-20 minutes. Peel off foil and break into pieces. Mixture will be light in color and frothy before done (let it get darker).

Kibbles n' Bits
Sallee Walker

3/4 c. margarine
1 1/2 c. peanut butter
12 oz. pkg. milk chocolate chips

Melt together until easily mixed (on stove or in microwave).

Add:

12 c. bite-sized crispy rice cereal squares
1 1/2 c. dry roasted peanuts

Mix chocolate mixture with cereal. Let stand for 5 minutes. Put in a large bowl with lid; add 3 cups of powdered sugar and shake together. Makes quite a lot ...a large bowlful.

Brownie Mix

Michelle Golz

4 c. flour
6 c. sugar
3 c. cocoa

4 t. baking powder
3 t. salt
2 c. vegetable shortening

Combine and mix well flour, sugar, cocoa, baking powder and salt. Using pastry blender thoroughly cut in vegetable shortening. Store in airtight container in cool dry place (can freeze, but bring up to room temperature before making). Yield: 8 batches.

To use mix:

2 c. mix
2 eggs

1 t. vanilla
1/2 c. chopped nuts (if desired)

Combine all ingredients; stir until moist. Spread in lightly greased 8" square pan. Bake in preheated 350 degree oven for 20-25 minutes, or until set in the center. Cut into 2" squares. Yield: 16 brownies.

Variations: Add 1 cup of chocolate chips, butterscotch chips, hot fudge sauce, caramel ice cream topping or chopped maraschino cherries.

Two-Tone Fudge

Karen Hayes

1 c. evaporated milk
2 c. sugar
1 lb. (14) caramels

3/4 c. semi-sweet
          chocolate morsels
1/2 c. peanut butter

Combine evaporated milk and sugar in 2-quart saucepan; add caramels. Place over low heat and cook, stirring constantly, until sugar is dissolved and mixture come to a boil. Increase heat and boil for 4 minutes, stirring constantly. To 1 1/2 cups of the mixture add chocolate morsels and stir until smooth. Turn into a greased 8" pan. To remaining mixture add peanut butter and stir until smooth. Turn into pan over chocolate mixture. Chill until firm and cut into squares. Yield: 2 lbs.

*Save a snowball in the freezer and in July,
get it out and remember all the Christmas fun you had!*

•Festive Food & Drink•

Microwave Fudge
Phyllis Purvis

16 oz. pkg. powdered sugar,
   sifted
1/2 c. cocoa
1/4 t. salt

1/2 c. butter or margarine
1/4 c. milk
1 T. vanilla flavoring
1/2 c. chopped pecans

Combine powdered sugar, cocoa and salt in a 2-quart glass bowl; add butter. Microwave on HIGH, uncovered, for 2 to 3 minutes; add milk, stirring until blended. Microwave on HIGH for 1 minute; stir in vanilla and nuts. Pour into lightly greased 8" square pan. Refrigerate until fudge is firm; cut into small squares. Yield: 1 1/2 lbs. fudge.

Peanut Brittle
Corinne McClellan

I was church secretary for several years, and a batch of this peanut brittle was my first Christmas gift to the pastor. He always hinted for his peanut brittle when it got close to Christmas. When he was transferred to a church in another city, he told the new pastor to remember to hint for peanut brittle for Christmas...which he did!!

2 c. sugar
1 c. dark corn syrup
1 c. water
1 lb. raw peanuts
2 T. butter or margarine

2 t. vanilla (pre-measure so
   it's ready to add quickly)
2 t. baking soda (pre-measure
   so it's ready to add quickly)

Mix sugar, corn syrup and water in a large kettle. Cook covered until mixture boils, then remove cover. From now on stir to prevent burning, using a wooden spoon. When temperature reaches 236 degrees, add peanuts. When temperature reaches 280 degrees, add butter or margarine. When temperature reaches 300 degrees, remove from heat and add vanilla and baking soda, stirring constantly. Pour immediately on a large (no sided) buttered cookie sheet. Do not try to spread too thin, peanut brittle is more crunchy if left a little thick. After peanut brittle hardens a few minutes, put a spatula under edges and loosen all around cookie sheet. Place in refrigerator for 30 minutes. When cool, remove and break into pieces and store in a covered container. This recipe may take a little longer to make than other peanut brittle recipes, about one hour from beginning to end...but it is well worth the extra time.

Kids' Krunch

Kim Estes

Like most families, ours loves to have sweet munchies around to pick up by the handful. But, like most kids, ours are constantly picking out the nuts, coconut and dried fruit, or what they think is "grown-up stuff." So, we concocted this creation just for kids...no grown-up stuff allowed!

1 stick margarine
1 c. brown sugar
1/2 c. dark corn syrup
1 box bite-size crispy rice cereal squares

Melt margarine, sugar and corn syrup in a saucepan. Pour over cereal, toss well. Bake on a cookie sheet or in a roasting pan at 250 degrees for 1 hour, stirring every 15 minutes. Pour on waxed paper to cool. Store in an airtight container.

•Festive Food & Drink•

Butter Nut Crunch Toffee

Joan Lachance

about 40 saltine crackers
1 c. butter, not margarine
1 c. brown sugar
12 oz. chocolate chips
1 c. crushed nuts

Place crackers (do not overlap) on a foil-lined cookie sheet. Melt butter in a saucepan; add brown sugar and boil for 3 minutes exactly, stirring constantly. Pour mixture over crackers, spreading all over the tops of crackers. Bake in 400 degree oven for 5 minutes. Take out of oven, sprinkle with chocolate chips; after 2 minutes, spread chocolate chips over top with the back of a spoon. Sprinkle crushed nuts evenly over the top. Cool in refrigerator for at least 2 hours. Cut with a sharp knife in long rows and then cut into pieces. Clean up is a snap because of the aluminium foil.

Frosted Pecans

B.J. Myers
Gooseberry Patch

1 lb. pecans
1/2 c. butter or margarine
1 c. sugar
2 stiffly beaten egg whites
pinch of salt

Toast pecans in 300 degree oven until light brown and crisp (about 15 minutes). Fold sugar and salt into egg whites. Fold pecans into meringue. Melt butter or margarine in sheet pan 13"x9"x2". Spread nut mixture over butter or margarine; bake slowly in 325 degree oven for 30 minutes, stirring every 10 minutes, until nuts are coated and no butter remains. Let cool and put into decorative tins or mason jars to give as yummy gifts.

Christmas Peppernuts

Sheryl Esau

1 c. butter or margarine
4 c. brown sugar
4 eggs, beaten
1 T. soda in 1 T. hot water
1 t. cinnamon

1 t. star anise, ground
1/2 t. nutmeg
1/4 t. cloves
3 c. nuts, chopped
7 c. flour

Cream shortening and sugar until fluffy. Add eggs, beating well. Add soda in water. Sift dry ingredients with spices and flour. Add half the amount of flour mixture to creamed mixture, mixing well. Add remaining flour; knead thoroughly. Add nuts. Store dough in tightly covered container in the refrigerator overnight or longer (this helps the dough to season and spices to blend). Roll dough into thin ropes and slice with a sharp knife dipped in flour or cold water (the smaller the better). Place pieces separately on greased baking sheet. Bake at 375 degrees for 7-10 minutes. When I have a lot of time and want to get fancy, I roll out the dough and use a 1" heart cookie cutter to make my peppernuts.

Glazed Spiced Pecans

Terri Burdoff

3/4 c. sugar
1 egg white
2 1/2 t. water
1/2 t. cinnamon
1/4 t. allspice

1/4 t. cloves
1/4 t. nutmeg
1/2 t. salt
8 c. pecans

Mix all ingredients in a large bowl. Spread onto a cookie sheet. Bake at 225 degrees for 30 minutes. Cool on waxed paper. Pack in airtight containers. Yield: 8 cups.

Grandma's Elderberry Cough Syrup Recipe "1876"

Juanita Williams

Take elderberries perfectly ripe, wash and strain, then put a pint of molasses to a pint of juice; boil 20 minutes, stirring constantly. When cold, add to each quart, a pint of French brandy. Bottle it and cork it tight. It's an excellent cough remedy and very tasty. (We bet Grandpa thought so too!)

Macadamia Mini-Loaves

Terri Rasmussen

3 1/2 oz. jar of macadamia nuts
1/3 c. flaked coconut
1 large lemon
3/4 c. butter or margarine
    (1 1/2 sticks), softened
3 c. all-purpose flour

1/2 c. milk
1 1/2 t. vanilla extract
1 t. baking powder
2 eggs
1 1/2 c. + 1 T. sugar

Finely chop enough macadamia nuts to measure 1/3 cup; set aside. Coarsely chop remaining nuts, place in a small bowl and stir in coconut and 1 tablespoon of sugar. From lemon: grate 2 teaspoons peel and squeeze 3 tablespoons juice. Preheat oven to 350 degrees. Grease and flour four 5 3/4"x 3 1/4" loaf pans or one 9" tube pan. In a large bowl, with mixer at high speed, beat butter and 1 1/2 cups sugar until light and fluffy. Add flour, milk, vanilla, baking powder and eggs, lemon peel and juice; at low speed, until just mixed, constantly scraping the bowl. Stir in the finely chopped macadamias. Spoon batter into pans. Sprinkle coconut mixture evenly over batter, then lightly press into batter. Bake small loaves 60 minutes or tube cake 1 hour 10 minutes, until toothpick inserted in center comes out clean. If topping begins to brown too quickly, loosely cover pans with foil. Cool cakes in pans on wire racks for 10 minutes; remove from pans; cool completely on racks. Makes 4 loaves, 4 servings each or 1 ring, 16 servings.

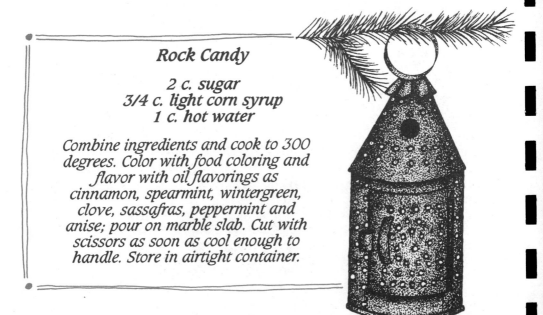

Rock Candy

2 c. sugar
3/4 c. light corn syrup
1 c. hot water

Combine ingredients and cook to 300 degrees. Color with food coloring and flavor with oil flavorings as cinnamon, spearmint, wintergreen, clove, sassafras, peppermint and anise; pour on marble slab. Cut with scissors as soon as cool enough to handle. Store in airtight container.

Cheese Bone Cookies for Dogs
Nancie Gensler

2 c. unsifted all-purpose flour
1 1/4 c. shredded cheddar cheese
2 cloves garlic, finely chopped

1/2 c. vegetable oil
4 to 5 T. water

Preheat oven to 400 degrees. Make a cardboard pattern of a dog bone, 4" long, or use a dog bone cookie cutter or trace a store-bought dog biscuit. Combine flour, cheese, garlic and vegetable oil in container or food processor. Cover; whirl until mixture is consistency of coarse meal. With machine running, slowly add water until mixture forms a ball. Divide dough into 12 equal pieces. Roll out each piece to 1/2" thickness. Cut out bones. Transfer to ungreased cookie sheet. Do not re-roll scraps. Bake for 10-15 minutes or until bottom of cookies are lightly browned. Carefully transfer bones to wire rack to cool completely. Refrigerate in airtight container. Makes 12- 4" cookie bones.

Healthy Dog Treats
Jacqueline Lash-Idler

Visiting in a dog lover's home? Bring along some homemade, easy to bake dog cookies. The dogs love them and you can boast about how healthy they are!

2 c. whole wheat flour
1/4 c. cornmeal
1/2 c. unbleached flour
   (or soy flour)
1/4 c. sunflower seeds
   (or pumpkin seeds)

1 t. salt
2 T. oil or butter
1/4 c. molasses
2 eggs, lightly beaten
1/4 c. milk

Mix all ingredients (add more milk if needed to make dough firm). Roll out onto a floured surface, to a 1/2" thickness. Bake on cookie sheets at 350 degrees for 30 minutes, until lightly toasted. To make biscuits harder, leave in oven with the heat turned off for an hour or more. Use any shape cookie cutter, but bone shape is most appropriate. Place the cookies in a plastic sandwich bag and tie with a festive ribbon.

Get all bundled up and have a skating party. Serve hot cocoa and cups of chili to warm everyone up!

INDEX

APPETIZERS
Bacon Treats, 128
Baked Baby Gouda, 129
Barbecue Meatballs, 125
Cheese Strips, 128
Cocktail Walnuts, 194
Crab Cheese Muffins, 131
Curried Crab Dip, 130
Grandma Muschweck's Cheeseball, 130
Hot Crab Dip, 129
Mushroom Turnovers, 124
Mushroom Rolls, 126
Onion Kuchen, 163
Open Face Cucumber Sandwiches, 132
Party Rye Appetizer, 125
Pizza Fondue, 125
Polish Mistakes, 131
Roasted Pumpkin Seeds, 13
Salsa, 127
Spiced Cream Cheese Spread, 130
Stefan's Cheese Ball, 128
Super Loaf, 131
Tangy Barbecued Meatballs, 126
Tennessee Caviar, 126
Tortilla Roll Ups, 127
Veggie Bars, 124

BEEF
Barbecue Beef, 23
Beef Hash, 146
Christmas Meatloaf, 149
Dinner-In-A-Pumpkin, 25
Meatballs and Sauerkraut, 150
Pot Roast Special, 152
Roast in Wine, 151
Those Harvest Meatballs, 24

BEVERAGES
Banana Crush Punch, 134
Bavarian Mint Coffee Mix, 195
Christmas Punch, 132
Cranberry Mist, 134
Holiday Cocoa, 200
Hot Spiced Tea, 133
Hot Buttered Rum, 133
Hot Cranberry Punch, 134
Indian Spiced Tea, 10
Mom's Cure-All Spice Tea Mix, 15
Mulling Spice Bags, 199
Raspberry Punch, 132
Spiced Cider, 133
Spiced Cider Mix, 17
Vanilla Coffee, 195

BREADS
Amy's Ap-peel-ing Apple Bread, 48
Applesauce Muffins, 136
Beer Bread, 49
Brad's "Great Pumpkin" Bread, 50
Broccoli Corn Bread, 47
Butternut Rolls, 48
Buttery Scones, 141
Colonial Brown Bread, 49
Cowboy Biscuits, 49
Easy Caramel Orange Ring, 137
Gift of the Magi Bread, 202
Grandmom Nellie's Christmas
   Eve Fried Dough, 136
Macadamia Mini-Loaves, 212
No Knead Pecan Rolls, 138
No Knead Yeast Butter Rolls, 47
Poppy Seed Bread, 199
Pumpkin Ribbon Bread, 53
Swedish Almond Braid, 198
Wonderful Sausage Bread, 138

BREAKFAST
Apple Fritters, 140
Breakfast Pie, 139
Christmas Morning Sticky Buns, 140
Gary's Sausage Gravy, 143
Glazed Cinnamon Breakfast Loaf, 144
Gramma's Cornmeal Pancakes, 144
Grandma Alta's Pancake Men, 141
Potato Pancakes, 144
Praline Pecan French Toast, 142
Sausage Cake, 142
Skiers French Toast, 139
Yummy Breakfast Rolls, 142

CAKES
14 Layer Chocolate Cake, 178
Apple Nut Dessert Cake, 53
Apple Cider Cake, 66
Aunt Libby's Rum Cake, 183
Gingerbread, 60
Grandma Mac's Banana Cake
   With Brown Sugar Frosting, 55
Italian Love Cake, 173
Mom's Carrot Cake, 57
Old-Fashioned Fruitcake, 184
Orange Spice Cake, 183
Peanut Butter Cake, 168
Pennsylvania Dutch Apple Muffin Cake, 61
Quick Coffee Cake, 137
Raisin Apple Harvest Cake, 56

CANDIES & CONFECTIONS
Becky's Caramels, 204
Butter Nut Crunch Toffee, 210
Candy Strawberries, 171
Caramel Apple Slice Dip, 61
Caramel Corn, 58
Cashew Brittle, 206
Chocolate Topped Toffee, 194
Christmas Peppernuts, 211
Creme de Menthe Squares, 170
Divinity, 202
Failproof Peanut Patties, 178
Frosted Pecans, 210
Glazed Spiced Pecans, 211
Heavenly Fudge, 205
Kibbles n' Bits, 206
Kids' Krunch, 209
Marshmallow Cut-Outs, 203
Microwave Fudge, 208
Peanut Butter Penuche, 194
Peanut Brittle, 208
Popcorn Balls, 52
Puppy Chow Snack (for people!), 202
Rock Candy, 212
Snowflake Pecans, 205
Sweet and Crunchy Walnuts, 204
Two-Tone Fudge, 207
White Chocolate Fudge, 204
Yummy Caramel Corn, 203

CASSEROLES
Apple Butternut Squash Casserole, 32
Broccoli Cheese Casserole, 158
Corn Casserole, 34
Country Dressing, 162
Harvest Dressing, 33
Hash Brown Potato Casserole, 160
Nanny Schantz's Turkey Dressing, 161
Reuben Casserole, 24
Sage Dressing, 159
Smoked Sausage Harvest Casserole, 23
Sweet Potato Casserole, 157
Vegetable Casserole, 34
Wild Rice Casserole, 35
Yankee Pleaser Casserole, 147
Zucchini Dressing Casserole, 158
Zucchini Casserole, 35

COOKIES
Applesauce Raisin Drops, 64
Buttermilk Cookies, 177
Coconut Macaroons, 185

German Lackerly Cookies, 174
Gingerbread Cookies, 180
Gram's Lemon Sugar Cookies, 172
Grandma Smith's Sugar Cookies, 173
Gumdrop Cookies, 168
Holiday Shortbread Drops, 175
Lollipop Cookies, 172
Me-Ma's Cookies, 177
My Three Sons' Christmas Cookies, 175
New Year Cookies, 174
Old-Fashioned Iced Sugar Cookies, 176
Pecan Fingers, 59
Pumpkin Cookies with
    Caramel Frosting, 64
Spicy Molasses Drop Cookies, 181

DESSERTS
Apple Grunt, 54
Apple Snow, 50
Brownie Mix, 207
Chocolate Torte, 174
Christmas Ice Cream, 179
Christmas Cheesecake, 186
Cranberry Candles, 155
Cranberry Cups, 154
Cranberry Dessert, 66
Death By Chocolate, 171
Easy Plum Pudding, 182
Easy Apple Dumplings, 16
Fall Pumpkin Squares, 56
Frosty Strawberry Squares, 188
Grama's Apple Crisp, 55
Hello Dollies, 186
Holiday Squares, 181
Holiday Cranberry Cobbler, 169
Indian Pudding, 65
Lemon Coconut Squares, 184
Millionaire Brownies, 169
Miniature Tea Pastries, 180
Mom Schantz's Walnut
    Pumpkin Pudding, 65
Old Timey Apple Brownies, 57
Pecan Cheesecake, 63
Poinsettia Desserts, 185
Pumpkin Layered Dessert, 58
Raisin Spice Bars, 63
Rice Pudding, 155
Snow Ice Cream, 188
Snow Pudding, 179
Spiced Peaches, 164
Yummy Baked Apples, 35

EGG DISHES
Harvest Quiche, 28
Overnight Egg Omelet, 143
Pickled Beet Eggs, 163

HAM
Baked Ham (with Cherry Glaze), 146
Stromboli, 147

JAMS, JELLIES, BUTTERS AND SAUCES
Apple Butter, 59
Citrus or Orange Butter, 201
Hot Pepper Jelly, 196
Maple Whipped Butter, 143
Orange-Cranberry Marmalade, 197
Raisin-Cranberry Sauce, 36
Susan's Pumpkin Butter, 195

PASTA
Curry Spinach Tortellini, 163
Easiest Lasagna, 151
Pasta Fagiola, 22
Pasta al Pesto, 22
Pasta Oil, 197

PETS
Cheese Bone Cookies for Dogs, 213
Healthy Dog Treats, 213

PIES
Betsye's Lemon Pie, 192
Butterscotch Pie, 192
Chewy Pecan Pie, 191
Egg Nog Pie, 190
French Apple Creme Pie, 191
Frozen Peanut Butter Pie, 189
Get Your Moose Chocolate Style (A real chocolate mousse pie, that is!), 187
Grandma Liz's Pumpkin Pie, 62
Grape Pie, 52
Not-So-Sweet Pecan Pie, 59
Paper Bag Apple Pie, 190
Pumpkin Ice Cream Pie, 62
Sour Cream Peach Pie, 189
The Best Apple Walnut Raisin Pie, 60

POULTRY
Baked Chicken Casserole, 148
Cheddar Chicken Pot Pie, 26
Chicken Breasts with Champagne Sauce, 149
Chicken Cheese Bake, 151
Chicken Divine, 150
Chicken-Rosemary Casserole, 26
Christmas Night Turkey Casserole, 149
Garden Chicken Casserole, 148
Sour Cream Tacos, 27

SALADS
Apricot Mold, 165
Broccoli Salad, 32
Caramel Apple Salad, 54
Christmas Buffet Potato Salad, 161
Christmas Fruit Salad, 166
Christmas Eve Salad, 159
Cranberry Salad Delight, 164
Cranberry Orange Salad, 31
Creamed Cucumber Salad, 33
Eggnog Fruit Salad, 165
Frozen Lime Mint Salad, 154
Hot Chicken Salad, 166
Raspberry Salad Wreath, 166
Harvest Salad, 30
Spiced Cranberry-Orange Mold, 160
Star Croutons, 50
Thyme, Lemon Peel & Black Pepper Vinegar, 200

SOUPS, CHOWDERS & STEWS
10 Bean Soup, 45
Beef Barley Soup, 42
Broccoli Cheese Soup, 38
Broccoli Crab Bisque, 46
Cheddar Chowder, 41
Clam Chowder, 40
Corn Chowder, 39
Easy Velvet Broccoli Soup, 39
Hearty Vegetable Chowder, 42
Old New England Cheddar Cheese Soup, 46
Potato Tuna Chowder, 43
Sausage Soup, 41
Shrimp Chowder, 40
The Famed Liz Martin's Marvelous Minestrone, 152
The Great Pumpkin Stew, 44
Tortilla Soup, 43
Williamsburg Turkey Soup, 38
Zucchini Sausage Soup, 45

VEGETABLES
Baked Potatoes and Broccoli, 157
Broccoli Curry, 161
Corn Custard, 30
Hardy 3-Bean Bake, 156
Holiday Potatoes, 158
Lentils and Rice, 32
Maple Candied Sweet Potatoes, 31
Old Settlers' Baked Beans, 30
Russian Mushroom Pie, 27
Swedish Green Potatoes, 162
Sweet Potato Pudding, 156

Yuletide Menus ☆ Open House ☆ Stocking Stuffers ☆ Memories ☆ Christmas Crafts ☆ Celebrations & Events ☆ My Wish List ☆ Memories ☆ Recipes ☆ Decorating ideas ☆ Holiday Hints ☆ Gift Lists ☆ Traditions ☆ Christmas Cards ☆

Yuletide Menus ☆ Open House ☆ Stocking Stuffers ☆ Memories ☆ Christmas Crafts ☆ Celebrations & Events ☆ My Wish List ☆ Memories ☆ Recipes ☆ Decora -ting ideas ☆ Holiday Hints ☆ Gift Lists ☆ Traditions ☆ Christmas Cards ☆

Yuletide Menus ☆ Open House ☆ Stocking Stuffers ☆ Memories ☆ Christmas Crafts ☆ Celebrations & Events ☆ My Wish List ☆ Memories ☆ Recipes ☆ Decorating ideas ☆ Holiday Hints ☆ Gift Lists ☆ Traditions ☆ Christmas Cards

Gooseberry Patch Originals

WELCOME HOME for the HOLIDAYS – Your companion from September through December

OLD-FASHIONED COUNTRY CHRISTMAS. Over 170,000 sold!

OLD-FASHIONED COUNTRY COOKIES. Hundreds of recipes, tips & ideas

FOR BEES & ME – Garden fresh recipes, backyard entertaining, & gifts from the garden

TEACUPS & GINGERBREAD, A Kitchen Journal – Warm, friendly, inviting... like a cozy country kitchen

SLEIGH BELLS & MISTLETOE, A Christmas Journal – Christmas all through the house

BUMBLEBEES & BUTTERFLIES, A Garden Journal ~ Blooming with magical illustrations, tips & ideas

GOOSEBERRY PATCH
27 N. Union Street
P.O. Box 190, Dept. **WELC**
Delaware, OH 43015

A Country Store In Your Mailbox®

How to Order
For faster service on credit card orders,
call toll·free 1-800-85-GOOSE!
(1-800-854-6673)

I would like to order the following Gooseberry Patch books:

How Many	Book	Item Price	Total
	Old-Fashioned Country Christmas	$14.95	
	Welcome Home for the Holidays	$14.95	
	Old-Fashioned Country Cookies	$14.95	
	For Bees & Me	$17.95	
	Teacups & Gingerbread, A Kitchen Journal	$10.95	
	Bumblebees & Butterflies, A Garden Journal	$10.95	
	Sleigh Bells & Mistletoe, A Christmas Journal	$10.95	

Merchandise Total _____

Ohio Residents Add 5 1/2% _____

Add $2 for each book for shipping & handling _____

Total _____

*Quantity discounts and special shipping prices available when purchasing
6 or more books. Call and ask! Wholesale inquiries invited.*

Name: _____

Address: _____

City: _____ State: _____ Zip: _____

We accept checks, money orders, Visa or Mastercard (please include expiration date).
Payable in U.S. funds only. Price subject to change.

GOOSEBERRY PATCH
27 N. Union Street
P.O. Box 190, Dept. **WELC**
Delaware, OH 43015

A Country Store In Your Mailbox®

How to Order
For faster service on credit card orders,
call toll·free 1-800-85-GOOSE!
(1-800-854-6673)

I would like to order the following Gooseberry Patch books:

How Many	Book	Item Price	Total
	Old-Fashioned Country Christmas	$14.95	
	Welcome Home for the Holidays	$14.95	
	Old-Fashioned Country Cookies	$14.95	
	For Bees & Me	$17.95	
	Teacups & Gingerbread, A Kitchen Journal	$10.95	
	Bumblebees & Butterflies, A Garden Journal	$10.95	
	Sleigh Bells & Mistletoe, A Christmas Journal	$10.95	

Merchandise Total _____

Ohio Residents Add 5 1/2% _____

Add $2 for each book for shipping & handling _____

Total _____

*Quantity discounts and special shipping prices available when purchasing
6 or more books. Call and ask! Wholesale inquiries invited.*

Name: _____

Address: _____

City: _____ State: _____ Zip: _____

We accept checks, money orders, Visa or Mastercard (please include expiration date).
Payable in U.S. funds only. Price subject to change.

GOOSEBERRY PATCH
27 N. Union Street
P.O. Box 190, Dept. WELC
Delaware, OH 43015

A Country Store In Your Mailbox

How to Order
For faster service on credit card orders,
call toll-free 1-800-85-GOOSE!
(1-800-854-6673)

I would like to order the following Gooseberry Patch books:

How Many	Book	Item Price	Total
_____	Old-Fashioned Country Christmas	$14.95	_____
_____	Welcome Home for the Holidays	$14.95	_____
_____	Old-Fashioned Country Cookies	$14.95	_____
_____	For Bees & Me	$17.95	_____
_____	Teacups & Gingerbread, A Kitchen Journal	$10.95	_____
_____	Bumblebees & Butterflies, A Garden Journal	$10.95	_____
_____	Sleigh Bells & Mistletoe, A Christmas Journal	$10.95	_____

Merchandise Total	_____	
Ohio Residents Add 5 1/2%	_____	
Add $2 for each book for shipping & handling	_____	
Total	_____	

*Quantity discounts and special shipping prices available when purchasing
6 or more books. Call and ask! Wholesale inquiries invited.*

Name: _____

Address: _____

City: _____ State: _____ Zip: _____

We accept checks, money orders, Visa or Mastercard (please include expiration date).
Payable in U.S. funds only. Price subject to change.

GOOSEBERRY PATCH
27 N. Union Street
P.O. Box 190, Dept. WELC
Delaware, OH 43015

A Country Store In Your Mailbox

How to Order
For faster service on credit card orders,
call toll-free 1-800-85-GOOSE!
(1-800-854-6673)

I would like to order the following Gooseberry Patch books:

How Many	Book	Item Price	Total
_____	Old-Fashioned Country Christmas	$14.95	_____
_____	Welcome Home for the Holidays	$14.95	_____
_____	Old-Fashioned Country Cookies	$14.95	_____
_____	For Bees & Me	$17.95	_____
_____	Teacups & Gingerbread, A Kitchen Journal	$10.95	_____
_____	Bumblebees & Butterflies, A Garden Journal	$10.95	_____
_____	Sleigh Bells & Mistletoe, A Christmas Journal	$10.95	_____

Merchandise Total	_____	
Ohio Residents Add 5 1/2%	_____	
Add $2 for each book for shipping & handling	_____	
Total	_____	

*Quantity discounts and special shipping prices available when purchasing
6 or more books. Call and ask! Wholesale inquiries invited.*

Name: _____

Address: _____

City: _____ State: _____ Zip: _____

We accept checks, money orders, Visa or Mastercard (please include expiration date).
Payable in U.S. funds only. Price subject to change.